Seen, Heard, and Valued

To my children, Spencer and Maisie, for lending your personal stories and thoughts on inclusive practices as contributions to this work. The lessons learned from you have taught and inspired me more than has any academic pursuit.

Seen, Heard, and Valued

Universal Design for Learning and Beyond

Lee Ann Jung

For information:

Corwin
A SAGE Company
2455 Teller Road
Thousand Oaks, California 91320
(800) 233-9936
www.corwin.com

SAGE Publications Ltd.
1 Oliver's Yard
55 City Road
London EC1Y 1SP
United Kingdom

SAGE Publications India Pvt. Ltd.
B 1/I 1 Mohan Cooperative
    Industrial Area
Mathura Road, New Delhi 110 044
India

SAGE Publications Asia-Pacific Pte. Ltd.
18 Cross Street #10-10/11/12
China Square Central
Singapore 048423

Artwork created by Taryl Hansen

Printed in Canada

ISBN 978-1-0718-4185-3

Library of Congress Cataloging-in-Publication Data

Names: Jung, Lee Ann, author.

Title: Seen, heard, and valued : Universal design for learning and beyond / Lee Ann Jung.

Subjects: LCSH: Inclusive education. | Educational sociology. | Educational equalization. | Learning strategies. | Grading and marking (Students)

Classification: LCC LC1200 .J87 2023 | DDC 371.9/046–dc23/eng/20220909

LC record available at https://lccn.loc.gov/2022040458

This book is printed on acid-free paper.

President: Mike Soules
Vice President and Editorial Director:
    Monica Eckman
Program Director and Publisher:
    Dan Alpert
Senior Content Development Editor:
    Lucas Schleicher
Content Development Editor:
    Mia Rodriguez
Editorial Assistant: Natalie Delpino
Production Editor: Vijayakumar
Copy Editor: Christobel Colleen
    Hopman
Typesetter: TNQ Technologies
Proofreader: Benny Willy Stephen
Indexer: TNQ Technologies
Cover Designer: Scott Van Atta
Marketing Manager: Melissa Duclos

23 24 25 26 27 10 9 8 7 6 5 4 3 2

Contents

Foreword

Inclusion and belonging are topics near to my heart. In fact, the first book I ever wrote was for the PEAK parent information center and it focused on inclusive practices for students with disabilities. The field of inclusive schooling practices has come a long way since then and I'm pleased to see universal design for learning taking center stage. Early on, advocates for inclusive schooling practices focused on creating accommodations and modifications for students with disabilities such that they could access the regular classroom. Today, we realize that classrooms must change to ensure that all students are successful.

I very much appreciate the central message of this book, namely "what's necessary for some is good for all." That motto is more than a platitude; it serves as the guiding philosophy of the book. The examples throughout the book allow educators to create changes such that a wide range of students benefit and the educational enterprise is improved.

There are a few things that make this book unique. First, Lee Ann mobilizes the Visible Learning database, providing effect sizes and information about the various influences that are used to provide evidence for each of the recommendations. In doing so, the suggestions are grounded in research and are harder to dismiss by individuals who are stuck in an outdated mental model of schooling.

Second, Lee Ann provides concrete examples of how to implement universal design for learning by exploring:

1. how we ***engage*** our students and sustain their interest and persistence,

2. how we ***represent*** our instruction in ways that are accessible, helps us connect with students and improves their understanding, and

3. how we give options to students for their ***expression*** of learning.

In doing so, Lee Ann uses a commonly known framework but breathes new life into it. The examples and activities help readers re-think the support they provide to all students and simultaneously ensure that the students who challenge us most are not neglected or forgotten. In fact, this is one of the great aspects of this book. Equitable and inclusive schooling requires that we embrace the variation that exists in our schools and build systems of support for all students to learn.

Third, Lee Ann tackles the assessment and grading question that has plagued inclusive schooling practices for decades. When I first began to support students with significant disabilities in regular high school classrooms in 1992, we were not sure what to put in the gradebook. Some educators said that it wasn't "fair" for the student to get a letter grade without some sort of mark to indicate that there were modifications provided to the curriculum. In fact, some argued that students who received a modified curriculum should not earn a high school diploma. And a few even suggested that they should not participate in graduation ceremonies because they did not demonstrate the same levels of success as other students. Having said that, none of them were arguing against students with disabilities being educated in regular classrooms, as was the case in many schools at the time. We just had a roadblock with grading. But that issue is solved in this book as Lee Ann provides options for students to demonstrate their understanding and offers suggestions for determining mastery of students' learning.

In short, this is a useful resource and one that allows us all to consider the systems of support we create. As the late Dr. Maya Angelou suggested, do the best you can until you know better. Then, when you know better, do better! The time is now; we do know better.

—Douglas Fisher

About the Author

Lee Ann Jung, PhD, is founder of Lead Inclusion, Clinical Professor at San Diego State University, and a consultant to schools worldwide. A former special education teacher and administrator, Lee Ann now spends her time in schools, working shoulder-to-shoulder with teams in their efforts to improve systems and practice. She has consulted with schools in more than 30 countries and throughout the United States in the areas of universal design for learning, inclusion, intervention, and mastery assessment and grading. Lee Ann is the author of 7 books to date, numerous journal articles, and book chapters on inclusion, universal design, and assessment. She serves on the advisory board for Mastery Transcript Consortium, as section editor of *The Routledge Encyclopedia of Education*, and on the editorial board member for several professional journals. In her community, Lee Ann is a board member for Life Adventure Center, a local nonprofit with a mission of healing for those who have experienced trauma.

Contact Lee Ann at www.leadinclusion.org and follow her on Twitter at @leeannjung.

Acknowledgments

I would like to acknowledge Nicole DeZarn, my friend and thought partner on all things inclusion. I thank her for all of her collaborations over the past 20 years, and specifically her additions to this book. The work wouldn't be the same without her rich and numerous contributions.

Introduction

To meet the needs of all *students, we have to meet the needs of* each *student.*

—*Johnny Collett*

WHY DO WE SUCCEED?

Whether you're a classroom teacher, an administrator, or a specialist, like a counselor, ELL teacher, or special education teacher, as an educator, you've chosen to devote your career to serve your world by educating young people. As a dedicated, service-oriented person, you look for ways to continually reflect and improve upon your practice and achieve higher outcomes with all of your students. And right now, you are carving out a bit of your own time to read about and reflect on ways to bring equity in outcomes to your classroom and school. In all likelihood, you aren't paid the salary you deserve, and your students probably don't thank you for your service, but by all other measures you are a successful, independent adult and vitally important to your community. Congratulations, and thank you for what you do! But how did you get here? Why did you succeed, while some of your peers struggle as adults? What was true of your circumstances and your efforts that caused you to arrive where you are today?

I remember as a child hearing stories of a community business owner bragging that he'd pulled himself out of poverty through tireless hard work. His family lived in abject poverty, but as a 19-year-old, without a high school education, he walked confidently into a bank, took out a loan, and started his own business—one that thrived in the small town until his retirement. In some ways, it's fortunate that this man had the confidence to believe he could succeed because without such a belief in his abilities, he would've never walked into the bank.

Living in poverty, this business owner wouldn't have described himself as being privileged. But he was white and male, and the year was 1959 in which the young man took out the small business loan in the Deep South. At that time, it's without a doubt that no Black teen would've been given such consideration. I'm pretty sure a Black teen wouldn't even have been welcomed inside the bank. Was it his effort or his privilege that gave him success? Should his hard work be discounted or minimized? Absolutely not.

But should he feel so arrogant as to believe it was solely his own efforts that created success, devoid of fortune, albeit seemingly imperceptible to him? Also, no. His effort contributed and was necessary, but without the context of privilege in which this effort was situated, no amount of hard work could have gotten him there.

The concepts of "internal locus of control" and "self-efficacy" are essential to understand as we think about successful outcomes. Internal locus of control is a person's belief that they have a great deal of control within themselves over what happens to them (Rotter, 1966). Self-efficacy is a person's belief that they have what it takes to make positive outcomes in their lives happen (Bandura, 1994). This business owner's internal locus of control and strong self-efficacy were instrumental in his success, but also played a role in his denying the privilege that gave him the *opportunity* to walk into the bank. Instead, he and others in the community harbored resentment toward others for lacking the ability to "pull themselves up by the bootstraps," blind to the lack of privilege afforded to many others living in poverty. Without the privilege of being a white male, he may not have gained the qualities of internal locus of control and self-efficacy that were active ingredients in his effort. In other words, his privilege not only opened doors for him but is likely an enormous contributor to why he even had the gumption to *try*.

As educators, we serve a student population who experiences the full gamut of support, risk, privilege, protection, trauma, and resilience. We wouldn't be in the field of education if we didn't believe we could meaningfully and significantly mediate how these experiences impact our students. Our entire purpose, almost universally, for choosing education as a career path is to "make a difference." To realize this purpose, we embrace our jobs as vastly broader than only teachers of content, and instead identify as *mentors* who guide young humans to successful adulthood. And each one of us, from preschool teacher to higher education professor, plays a role in the chain of nurturing and adding to positive and protective factors students experience. But, frankly, "making a difference" is not measured in the performance of students who were going to succeed anyway. The most substantial difference is measured in our minority subpopulations of students, including our BIPOC students, LGBTQIA+ students, those who are new to the language of instruction, students with learning differences, those experiencing poverty, students who need behavioral support, those with disabilities, students who have had poor previous instruction, and those who have endured trauma. And we make a difference when we see, name, and diligently work to minimize marginalization in our school community for all subpopulations.

In your school, are each of these subgroups of students engaging, trying, and achieving at the same level as the full student population? Do they all have a sense of inclusion and belonging in the school community? Do they have an internal locus of control and strong self-efficacy? If not, there is an opportunity and an obligation to understand where the inequities are and to devote resources as a school to grow the equity and inclusion therein.

SELF-EFFICACY

d=.65

-1.00   0.0   1.50

Throughout the book, we use dials like the one here to connect to Hattie's research (Hattie, 2016) on the influences in education on students' outcomes, focusing on those influences that have the potential to accelerate learning, or those with an effect size (Cohen's d) above .40. Cohen's d is expressed in terms that are similar to a standard deviation. So, the influence of self-efficacy has an effect size of .65, then that influence makes 65% of a standard deviation difference in the child's learning. This difference is one that matters!

Without an actionable course, calls for a whole-child approach, equity, and inclusion have only the weight of platitudes. The purpose of this book is to take these broad and lofty terms and outline specific strategies for educators to intentionally bring equity in learning outcomes to their classrooms, schools, and systems. We are going to dig into the research on the reasons that students engage and persist and succeed and pair this research with universal practices for every classroom to connect with and reach each student and meet their needs. Through case stories and examples, you will reflect deeply on classroom and school practices and how to engage and support each student along a path to lifelong learning. We will follow Ms. Talbert as she works to increase the equity in her classroom.

REFLECTION

When you think back to your childhood, you can certainly identify contributing factors that led you to do well in school, to graduate, and go on to attend college. Were there certain people and events or conditions that affected your success? What were the challenges that got in your way at times? When you encountered tough times in your life, what, or who, helped you get through that and to persist toward your goal? What are your own, innate and learned qualities that shaped you into a successful adult? Is your success something that you created mostly through hard work, or do you see chance and other outside influences as a big part of your achievement? How might your success have changed if your demographics were different?

_____

_____

_____

_____

_____

CHAPTER ONE

Planning for Variability

Variability Is a Natural Part of the Human Condition

Learning Intentions	Success Criteria
I am learning about the false dichotomies that are present around us and how that has impacted how students are served.	I can give examples of dichotomies we use in speaking about characteristics of people and explain why these are false dichotomies.
I am learning about student variability and its effects on how we facilitate academic and social-emotional instruction and support.	I can describe the many types of student variability and how these affect the way I teach or provide support.
I am learning about what the research says about how we can improve our instruction to meet the needs of more learners.	I can use evidence from research to support the need for universal design for learning (UDL).
I am learning about the role of UDL in the first tier of Multi-Tiered System of Support (MTSS).	I can articulate why in the use of universal design for learning, intervention isn't the place to start.

Every classroom is filled with amazing individuals who vary wildly and interestingly in who they are as people. Their many experiences and genetics make them who they are—each one unique and wonderful. We have students with different racial and ethnic backgrounds, various cultural backgrounds, and differing family and social experiences. There is neurodiversity, variability in gender identity, sexual orientation, and varying degrees of family support for students who are LGBTQIA+. Students in our classrooms have experienced varying degrees of trauma, some for whom you will never even know have experienced this. Students vary in their preferences, strengths, skill levels, and interests in the academic content. Some students are strong with math, others are talented artists, some light up when it is time for science, and others love nothing more than to get lost in the world a fictional work. For every student who loves science, there is another who is afraid of it, and another who finds it uninteresting. Some students read many grade levels ahead, and some have dyslexia. Some students speak multiple languages but struggle in the language of instruction that is new to them. Students also vary in their social-emotional skills, development, and learning. Classrooms include students who persist for long periods of time, as well as students who give up if they believe learning is too hard. There are students who are confident in their ability to learn and those who are discouraged and struggle to believe they can succeed. There are students who move easily between activities, classrooms, and content areas, and others who have great difficulty with these transitions. Each of the aforementioned and all other areas of diversity are ever present and ***normal***.

This diversity of strengths and interests in our classrooms and what makes students who they are is an asset! There is power in our diversity. This diversity presents the opportunity for students to learn from and with one another, to gain an understanding of the interdependence within society, and to see and celebrate one another's unique qualities. This diversity is in no way a limitation as long as we design our instruction and assessment with this variability in mind. Our planning for variability is a celebration of the collective experiences our group shares because of this diversity. Honoring and celebrating diversity means that we reject models of instruction that are oriented toward the experience of the majority, as these traditional models marginalize every student in our class who doesn't fit that mold. Instead, we plan our instruction so that it's flexible enough to perfectly fit the needs of each student in our class. And this diversity creates the space and imperative for us to grow as teachers, honing our practice to facilitate success and belongingness of *all* our students. It's time we widen our view of "normal" to include the *full range* of our students. *Every student is normal in every way, because variation is normal.*

EVERYTHING IS A SPECTRUM

There was a time in the not-too-distant past when the predominate beliefs of the general public was that most human conditions fit into specific categories, often dichotomies—false dichotomies. Examples of this simplistic and misinformed thinking include gender, sexual orientation, neurodiversity, extraversion, and race as having clearly distinct categories: you were either straight or gay, you were either male or female, you were an introvert or an extravert, and you either had a disability or you didn't. Even race within the sociology textbooks was incorrectly thought of as being distinct categories of white, Black, and Asian. But this is not the way the human condition works! Variation is universal.

Interestingly, the fields of psychology and education view autism spectrum disorders (ASD) as just that: a spectrum with much variability. But really, *all* human conditions are also expressed on a spectrum. Gender, sexual orientation, ability, extraversion, and race, and the like include a continuum with gradations, not simply defined in categories. The way schools have traditionally conceptualized neurodiversity as dichotomous, combined with the strong focus on academic support, often to the exclusion of other types of support, have created enormous gaps in meeting the needs of *each* student. Meeting the needs of *all* students does not mean *most students*; it means *each student.*

Support Driven by Dichotomies and Labels

Until the mid-2000s, the way additional academic support was delivered to students in most schools largely hinged upon labels. If a student met the eligibility criteria to have an Individualized Education Program (IEP) because of a learning disability, for example, then that student received interventions and supports to address the learning disability. For students who were struggling to learn to read but did *not* have an IEP, though, no special education services were available. The same was true if a student's IQ score was too high to have an intellectual disability label and an IEP. Labels had clear dichotomous definitions, and a student either qualified completely or didn't qualify at all. But do you know of students who narrowly missed qualifying for an IEP? Do you know students who didn't quite fit the criteria for specific learning disability? Or ASD? Have you ever known a student whose academic performance was affected by depression but did not qualify for an IEP? Of course! We all do.

This distinction between who qualified for services and supports and who didn't was designed in the 1970s as a way to protect students with disabilities and ensure they received the supports they needed to access a free and appropriate public education. These are important rights provided to students, but this often doesn't coincide with needs. Therefore, the labels sometimes have led to exclusion and a parallel system that prevented many students from equitable access and learning. What was missing was an understanding that qualifying for an IEP, or living in poverty, or being new to the language of instruction is not synonymous with needing support in school. But until the idea of differentiation caught on and became standard best practice, the idea was to teach to the large group, and for students who struggled, there must be a need or problem with the student—not a need or problem with the instruction.

We all know that a student may benefit from academic intervention and not fit within a traditionally marginalized population, and students don't necessarily need academic intervention because they are a member of any demographic group. But for a long time, the system did not have a way to deliver support and intervention to any students except those with IEPs. So, students who did not fit the disability definitions oftentimes couldn't access supports, were tracked into "lower level" courses, or were inappropriately labeled as having a disability.

Historically, the flow of funding simply didn't allow for what now is seen as the common-sense approach: providing intervention to any student who needs it. And students who need support do not automatically need a label. Also, we don't wait to provide intervention until a student is significantly behind grade level. If a student is at risk for reading failure, we don't wait and see how that goes, but rather provide intervention *now*.

Further, academic support is not the only type of support our students need. Many times, a student who seems to need intervention with learning doesn't need academic support at all. For those who are lagging behind academically because of being new to the language of instruction, anxiety, lack of belonging, stress of living in poverty, depression, trauma, and the like, the solution is much more complex than, for example, delivering a reading intervention. Students need to be in an environment that is safe, embraces diversity of all kinds, one that is engaging and accessible, promotes belonging, and celebrates the many ways students can show their skills and understanding—no single way is "right" or "best."

An additional way that the dichotomous thinking and parallel systems have affected students is the settings in which students receive support. It remains true today that students who have IEPs and students who are novices in the language of instruction are frequently given support in a setting that is separate from the classroom to which they belong (National Council on Disability, 2018). Students are given support in resource rooms for students who have IEPs, in separate ELL rooms, and even when "included" in classrooms, it's often the case that students with these needs are seated together and given support by a paraprofessional/classroom assistant who is devoted to that group.

In this noninclusive scenario, students who have needs are segregated, and students without IEPs or an ELL label who need support can slip through the cracks. I work in schools all the time who want to make this change and are looking for next steps. We will delve into this inclusion challenge deeply, with alternative models of delivering support inclusively in Chapter 6 on flexible support.

TWO CORNERSTONE RESEARCH FINDINGS

Don't Use Labels as Passports to Support

During the 1990s, the research on various academic interventions continued to grow, and two important lessons were learned that would shape the trajectory of education quickly. First, more and more researchers validated the idea that delivering intervention by label wasn't the secret to success, but rather delivering support by *need* was really the answer. In other words, grouping all the students who have ASD together to teach social skills didn't make as much sense as grouping all the students who had the need for that particular social skills support. Not all students who have the need for the intervention have ASD, and not all students who have ASD needed that social skills support. Thus, this focus on labels as the passport to support is not effective (not labeling students: $d = .61$).

NOT LABELING STUDENTS

d=.69

-1.00   0.0   1.50

The same is true for students with language needs, emotional needs, or any other need. In fact, lots of students need extra support in learning to read, and only a small portion of those students have a neurological difference that we call specific learning disability. For many students having difficulty learning to read there is an environmental explanation, such as being new to the language of instruction, social-emotional needs, low literacy exposure, or—we don't like to admit this one—poor previous instruction. The good news is that the academic intervention that works for the student who does have a learning disability also works for almost any student who needs reading intervention. Our focus has also, traditionally, landed squarely on these *academic* needs. But we have all seen the awakening in schools in recent years to see the critical importance of social-emotional development. There is now an intense demand for resources to promote social-emotional development in our students.

Use a Multi-Tiered System of Support

The second important lesson from this line of research was that we can accomplish exponential results if we bring some of our strategies that were once reserved for special education and school counseling into all classrooms using a Multi-Tiered System of Support. Most special educators will tell you that they may or not be experts on any given content area, but rather are experts in pedagogy. Special educators and counselors will tell you that many strategies and skills they use are ones that can benefit all students in the school. And that's what the research continued to show. If we use these strategies with all students, fewer students need special interventions. The use of mnemonics is a good example of this. Using mnemonics is an evidence-based special education strategy that pairs something simple to remember (like an acronym or phrase) with something larger or more difficult to remember. From music, do you remember "Every Good Boy Does Fine"? EGBDF as letters on a scale are difficult to remember at first, but with the sentence, it's much easier to recall. Well, we don't only use this strategy in special education—it's something lots of teachers use to facilitate memory. Graphic organizers, a strategy probably every elementary and middle-school teacher uses, also have their roots in special education.

RESPONSE TO INTERVENTION

d=1.09

-1.00   0.0   1.50

This research, primarily out of the early reading research and learning disability research, formed what we now know as Response to Instruction and Intervention (RTI[2]). In 2004, with the reauthorization of the Individuals with Disabilities Act (2004), the compelling research on systems of intervention and support finally made its way into legislation. Soon after, the acronym RTI[2] began to infiltrate the language in schools across the United States. Books and conferences popped up seemingly weekly to assist schools in quick-start success with this newer way of approaching support. As to be expected, with the variability in implementation and context came variability in success.

The Multi-Tiered System of Support (MTSS) framework is one that guides decision-making and has a primary goal of *prevention* of poor outcomes (National Center on Response to Intervention, 2010). The most important component of the MTSS framework is its foundation—the practices we put into place in *every* classroom with *every* student. Using this model of making decisions about how to enhance our classroom instruction, intervene when needed, and increasing the intensity of intervention has an enormous impact on student outcomes (response to intervention: $d = 1.09$). But the focus often shifts to intervention first, rather than investing heavily in the foundation.

Although RTI[2] has its roots in academic support, researchers and schools began expanding this decision-making model to a broader spectrum of needs. MTSS give us a decision-making model for all types of supports, including social-emotional support. Such a focus in schools expands our priorities beyond academics and acknowledges that mental health, strong social skills, and emotional well-being are critical to teaching and developing young people who are happy, healthy, belong, and successful in a variety of ways. Remember the role that internal locus of control and self-efficacy that contributed to the business owners' and your success? A concerted effort to develop these qualities in our students changes their lives.

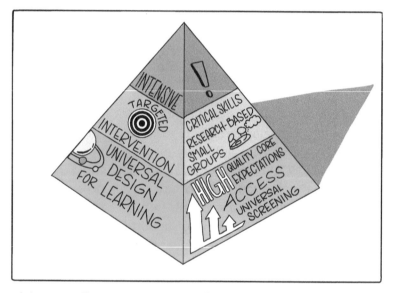

MULTI-TIERED SYSTEMS OF SUPPORT

One of the most common requests I get from schools as a consultant is to teach faculty tiers two and three strategies. Schools want to know how to deliver powerful interventions to students who are struggling in the classroom, regardless of why. That's fantastic! But it also isn't the starting place. In the rush to implement the models of intervention that accompany RTI[2], the very foundation of the model is often forgotten—that second part of the research that teaches us how to gain exponential effects by changing what we do in *every* classroom. RTI[2] is more about what we are doing in every classroom than it is about how we take data and intervene. Implementing RTI[2] means creating warm, inclusive, welcoming, environments that deliver the highest quality instruction and respond with intervention when the instruction isn't fully successful with a student.

REFLECTION

Think about a group of students you currently teach or know. Which ones have needs that would or do "fall through the cracks" of the older dichotomous thinking about support being only for students who meet the eligibility requirements of having an IEP? Who are the students in your class you worry about in quiet moments of reflection? Which of these have IEPs? Are there any students with any unmet social-emotional needs? Academic needs? Make a list of these students, and complete this prompt.

_____

_____

_____

_____

_____

STUDENT	IF THIS STUDENT COULD ONLY DO _____, IT WOULD CHANGE THEIR LIFE FOREVER

UNIVERSAL DESIGN FOR LEARNING

Next time you walk around town, take a look at all the ramps around you. They're at the entrances and within buildings, outside between sidewalks and the street, and in some homes. In the United States, this accessibility feature is required by law in public spaces. Without ramps, people who need wheelchairs or other mobility equipment are unable to move about town easily. When I travel to other countries that don't have accessibility laws, I don't see many people who use wheelchairs. We can find the same problem in historic buildings even in countries, like the United States, where accessibility laws are in place. In my own town, I've had conversations with people who use wheelchairs and heard the frustrations over wheelchair accessibility. One story that sticks out in my mind is of a friend who felt the most comfortable with a particular gym and trainer because the trainer figured out how to make excellent modifications to the workout movements. The problem was that the bus didn't go all the way to the gym, the sidewalk was uneven, and there were breaks in the crosswalk ramps. We all want independence, and yet my friend depended on other people to be able to access his accessible gym.

WHAT'S NECESSARY FOR SOME
IS GOOD FOR ALL.

Crosswalk ramps are a necessity for people who use wheelchairs to cross the street. But people who use wheelchairs are not the only people who benefit from crosswalk ramps, right? Can you think of a time when you benefited from a crosswalk ramp? Sure you can! Did you think of these: riding a bike, roller skating, pushing a stroller, pulling a suitcase, delivering something with a hand truck. Once I was teaching a class on this, and someone answered the question with, "short dogs benefit." Funny, and true. We *all* use ramps on a regular basis. The lesson here is "what is necessary for a few is helpful to many."

The single most important first step to designing for equity and inclusion is deep, sustained work on the instruction that all students get in every classroom. I'm not talking about the individualized instruction that we give to some students, but the instruction that is universal—the general curriculum offered in our school. Our goal is to design classroom environments and instruction that are so welcoming, kind, responsive, inclusive, accommodating, supportive, and flexible, that no student feels unrepresented or disregarded, and the fewest students possible need special intervention and support. And when students need intervention and support, we want our classrooms to be so effective that intervention is rarely needed long term. "Delivering high-quality core instruction" is a ubiquitous phrase in any MTSS work or initiative, but the "how-to" and investment into what that means for classroom planning has to be fully developed for this most important part of MTSS to be solid.

Universal Design for Learning, or UDL, is a framework conceptualized by the organization, CAST, that guides proactive design of core classroom instruction and learning opportunity in a way that is effective for a broad range of learners (www.cast.org). The principles of the UDL framework challenge us to plan (1) how we ***engage*** our students and sustain their interest and persistence; (2) how we ***represent*** our instruction in ways that are accessible, helps us connect with students, and improves their understanding; and (3) how we give options to students for how they their ***express*** their learning. Through the three principles of engagement, representation, and expression, we plan for the diversity within our classrooms by removing barriers to access learning. Many of the strategies in this book may cause you to think, "that's just good teaching." This is true! But the conceptual framework brings *intentionality* to our selection and use of strategies for the purpose of welcoming and meeting the needs of students with all types of variability within our classrooms with inclusion and equity. And with this intentional focus on the principles, we can always find specific ways to improve the reach of our instruction.

IS UDL DIFFERENTIATION?

Not all buildings were built with accessibility in mind. Those historic buildings that were built many decades or centuries ago, weren't designed to accommodate people who use wheelchairs. And to renovate a historic building to become accessible is a time-consuming and extraordinarily expensive operation. The same is true for accessibility of streets. The age and economic strength of a city or town are predictors of these features. But building a city or building with these design features from the outset of the planning is second nature at this point, requiring no more creativity or problem-solving than is required for the whole project.

Both UDL and differentiation respond to student variability. But UDL departs from differentiation in two important ways: When accessibility features are designed and for whom they are intended.

> **UDL** is a part of our initial lesson planning as strategies we use for all students, based on *predictable* variability we find in our classrooms year after year. The strategies are designed to be used year after year (Ralabate, 2016).

> **Differentiation** is added after lessons are designed and are intended to meet the needs of individual students in our class at a given time. Similar strategies may be used in the future, but they are individualized and applied for specific students (Tomlinson, 2014).

Differentiating with individual accommodations and modifications remain important components to an equitable classroom. But because instruction works best when we plan for *all* students and are agile to make changes when needed for *each* student, UDL and differentiation work in concert. Just like building design in which planning ahead is easier than renovations, universal design for learning is easier than differentiation. An investment in UDL makes our jobs easier in the long run.

There are many examples of universal design around us, our smartphones being a prime example. Fifteen years ago, you may have had a phone, a camera, a calculator, a video recorder, an audio recorder, a calendar, device for listening to music, a computer to browse online. If you traveled, you may have used GPS, or a map, and maybe books for translating languages. Perhaps you had all 11 of these items. But now, all of these needs are met with one device that most people already have. Because we have a customizable device with many options and functions, fewer people need something special. Sure, professional photographers still need highly technical cameras, and maybe you still prefer a physical calendar, but we would be hard pressed to find many people who own and use all 11 of those specialized items.

Think of UDL as the base design for our instruction—the smartphone with all the usual features and apps. UDL is the foundation for the entire classroom design. Our differentiated instruction is how we enhance that base design as needed—the specific additional apps and customization we add for a specific individual or group. Without UDL, we are left exhausted, trying to continually figure out how to differentiate and deliver support to meet individual needs and maximize strengths. By investing effort in UDL, we minimize special adaptations, because it was designed up front to work for many types of variability. Within a UDL framework, we have student variability in mind as we plan our instruction. In doing so, we embed the most high-leverage practices within every lesson in order to cast a broad net and meet the greatest possible needs. Instead of designing to the average, we "design to the edges" (Rose, 2016).

CASE STORY

Monica Talbert pondered the upcoming unit she was teaching in her senior social studies class. In the past, she'd been focused on the assignment, which was for students to write a paper. As she thought through what was most salient about this assignment, the essence of what was most important that students were able to do, she identified that her primary learning intention was that students learned to use evidence to support a claim. Although there was much more that she was teaching and that students were learning this was the essential skill she wanted every student in the class to have. Ms. Talbert was teaching her students this skill within the context of an advanced social studies course, but she wanted her students use this skill in all subjects and outside of school and across time. Many people require this skill in their careers, and everyone needs it just in life on a daily basis. Ms. Talbert was confident, that this is a worthwhile skill to teach.

As Ms. Talbert thought about the successes and challenges of students' writing their research papers in the past, she recounted many students who had incredible skills at persuasive speech because they truly had a deep understanding, not only of how to support a claim with evidence, but also of how to use evidence effortlessly within informal conversation. Looking back, she could see that these students, some of whom did not perform well on the written paper, had developed skills that far surpassed what most students achieved during the course. For some of the students who performed poorly on the paper, their speaking skills were at a level much higher than their writing skills. This was particularly true for several students who had IEPs she could remember, but was also true for many more. Ms. Talbert remembered Juan, who was in her class 4–5 years ago. English was a new language for Juan, and he had a hard time with the paper. But he was incredibly engaged in the content, had strong opinions, and he was able to adeptly support his opinions with evidence.

Ms. Talbert reflected on the profile of learners in her class this year relative to this skill. She made a list of students and jotted down strengths, interests, preferences, and needs for the students in her class relative to tasks and skills in the upcoming unit.

UNIT: SUPPORT A CLAIM WITH EVIDENCE	
Learning Intentions	**Success Criteria**
☐ I am learning how to research for information to support or refute a claim. ☐ I am learning to determine whether a source is credible.	☐ I can use multiple resources online to identify information relative to a claim. ☐ I can evaluate and determine the relative credibility of a source.

Student	Strengths	Interests and Preferences	Needs
Charlene	☐ Has confidence as a reader ☐ Has skills in using online resources to research ☐ Has a strong personality when speaking	☐ Prefers young-adult fiction ☐ Enjoys writing about personal experience ☐ Does not prefer speaking in front of the whole class	☐ Greater confidence in writing about nonfiction topics ☐ Finding a writing voice for persuasion ☐ Further development in organization and clarity
DeShawn	☐ Is confident with online research ☐ Has a strong vocabulary ☐ Has a developing voice in writing	☐ Prefers fantasy as a genre ☐ Prefers fiction writing about others (not himself)	☐ Developing persistence for engaging in nonfiction social studies work ☐ Further development in discerning the credibility of sources
Germaine	☐ Persists for long periods of time in reading and writing ☐ Has strong organization, vocabulary use, and clarity in writing ☐ Is confident with online research	☐ Enjoys reading about current events ☐ Interested in popular culture and psychology	☐ Engaging in broader social studies content ☐ Further development in discerning the credibility of sources
Jayson	☐ Is social and enjoys interacting with everyone in the class. ☐ Makes choices when given a few options	☐ Enjoys hearing short stories about people	☐ Naming people ☐ Using a pencil grasp when writing
Maciel	☐ Has a quirky humor in one-on-one conversation or with people he knows well	☐ Does not prefer speaking in front of other students ☐ Enjoys reading about current events from around the world ☐ Interested in nature and science topics	☐ Greater confidence in writing ☐ Increased organization and clarity in writing ☐ Stronger voice in writing ☐ Support with reading and writing in English

(Continued)

(Continued)

Next, Ms. Talbert developed a class profile by summarizing the class strengths, interests/preferences, and needs. The class profile includes each item from the student profile, but listed only once.

CLASS PROFILE SUMMARY		
Strengths	**Interests and Preferences**	**Needs**
☐ Some have confidence in writing, but most do not. ☐ Some have a strong vocabulary. ☐ A few have strong research skills. ☐ Many have confidence in reading. ☐ Some have organization and clarity in their writing. ☐ Some have strong personality or humor in conversation in small groups or with familiar people. ☐ Some are confident speaking in front of others.	☐ There are preferences for both fiction and nonfiction. ☐ There are preferences for science and nature, fantasy, and popular culture and psychology. ☐ Several prefer small group and one-on-one conversations. ☐ Some prefer writing about themselves, others prefer writing about others.	☐ Most need greater confidence in writing. ☐ Many need increased organization and clarity in writing. ☐ A few need support with reading. ☐ A few need support with reading and writing in English. ☐ Many need to develop skills in research. ☐ Some need to further develop their writing.

As she continued to think about her students from years past, Ms. Talbert noticed that although the names change each year, there is always much of the same variability in her students. She thought about types of variability beyond academic variability in all the students she had in all of her classes. There was variability in race, gender identity, sexual orientation, and intellectual ability. There were four students she knew had experienced significant trauma, six who had social anxiety, ten who had IEPs for learning disabilities, and twelve who were newer to English. The strengths, preferences, interests, and needs spanned the spectrum of possibilities. Yes, there was nothing about this profile that was unique to the students she listed or to this academic year. What incredible variability there was!

Ms. Talbert realized that the requirements of the paper for the upcoming unit kept more than a handful of students each year from showing the depth of their understanding and skills. Through this exercise she realized there were certain changes she could no doubt make in her lessons to respond to this variability she could expect year after year.

ACTION

Student variability does not involve dividing students by category or label. Labels are not the key to understanding variability. What matters are individual strengths, preferences, interests, priorities, and needs. To create a class profile, we begin by listing these unique qualities for each student. Because any individual's list of strengths, preferences, interests, priorities, and needs is lengthy, it can be helpful to focus on these relative to upcoming learning. First, select an upcoming unit you are planning and record the learning intentions and success criteria for one lesson. Next, choose ten students to consider and include the strengths, interests, and preferences for each student relative to the upcoming learning.

LESSON:			
Learning Intentions		**Success Criteria**	
Student	**Strengths**	**Interests and Preferences**	**Needs**

Next, develop a class profile for the upcoming unit by summarizing the class strengths, interests/preferences, and needs relative to the upcoming learning intentions and success criteria. List each item from the student profile only once.

(Continued)

(Continued)

LESSON:	
Learning Intentions	**Success Criteria**

CLASS PROFILE SUMMARY		
Strengths	**Interests and Preferences**	**Needs**

Because we can *assume* learner variability in every class, we can implement equitable and inclusive strategies without cataloging individual students' strengths, preferences, interests, and needs. But creating a class profile now will (1) help you explore the concept of variability and each of the principles of UDL within the context of students you have right now and (2) allow you to connect your universal instruction and individualized differentiation efforts later.

REFLECTION

As you examine the profile of learners for this unit, what do you notice? If you compare this group of learners to other groups you have had in the past, what are the similarities and contrasts? What are themes of learner strengths and needs you see year after year? How do you plan ahead for the patterns of needs you see each year?

_____

_____

_____

_____

_____

SUMMARY

In some ways, it's natural to think in dichotomies and categories in grouping and sorting, even with people. But this way of thinking is overly simplistic and, in our schools, can cause a major disconnect between our practices and the strengths and needs students have. Dichotomies are not the way the human condition works. Thus, our services cannot be delivered dichotomously to "students who have needs" and "those who don't." Every student has needs! We have to look not only at individual students, but *within* individual students and respond to each one's strengths, interests, and needs. As overwhelming as that can feel to any educator, we know this is the goal—to meet the needs of all by meeting the needs of each. UDL, situated within an MTSS framework offers us hope in truly maximizing the equity in our educational practices, and outcomes for students.

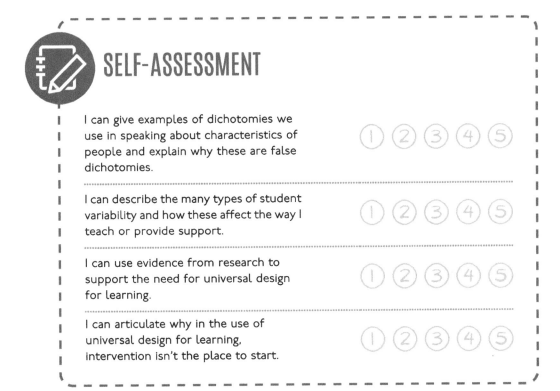

SELF-ASSESSMENT

I can give examples of dichotomies we use in speaking about characteristics of people and explain why these are false dichotomies. ① ② ③ ④ ⑤

I can describe the many types of student variability and how these affect the way I teach or provide support. ① ② ③ ④ ⑤

I can use evidence from research to support the need for universal design for learning. ① ② ③ ④ ⑤

I can articulate why in the use of universal design for learning, intervention isn't the place to start. ① ② ③ ④ ⑤

CHAPTER TWO

Emotionally Safe Environments

Create Environments Where Students Feel Welcomed and Empowered

Learning Intentions	Success Criteria
I am learning about becoming intentionally inviting in my classroom.	I can describe the elements of invitations and implement strategies to be intentionally inviting in my classroom.
I am learning specific ways students are excluded and harmed in the educational system.	I can describe ways that students in minority populations in categories of ability, gender identity, sexual orientation, and race experience harm and exclusion.
I am learning about how to establish a collaborative classroom culture in which everyone's voice is heard, protected, and barriers and risks are minimized.	I can identify and put into place specific strategies to establish an emotionally safe classroom.

It's important to acknowledge that this chapter barely touches the surface of dispositions, reflections, and actions to value diversity of all kinds and protect those who are harmed by exclusion and hate. To be truly welcoming of all groups requires careful reflection of the biases we each hold—and we all do. Regardless of how informed, empathetic, and "in-the-know" each of us feels we are on the complexities of diversity, equity, inclusion, and justice, we really are in our infancy as a society, and as individuals, in this work. In fact, in many ways, *because* we need to advocate for the erasure of exclusion, hate, and discrimination hurled at specific groups of humans shows we are only at the starting line. This chapter offers the most basic but important steps we can take in our classrooms to embrace, value, validate, and protect each of our students.

THE FEELING OF EXCLUSION

Take a minute to imagine yourself as an elementary student in a classroom where everyone is celebrating an upcoming religious holiday, but it isn't one that your family celebrates. Think about how you would feel as a middle-school student in a classroom in which you are the only person in that classroom, including your teacher, with your skin color. Imagine yourself being new to the language of instruction as an incoming high school student. How would you feel if you were in a highly competitive environment, but you were struggling to keep up? Perhaps some of these are your own experience, or maybe you've never had any of these experiences. No amount of *imagining* exclusion can produce the emotions of experiencing the feeling of being different and excluded. And being excluded on occasion in no way can compare to the cumulative trauma that builds over time from being excluded over and over because of race, religion, ability, sexual orientation, or gender identity. Reflecting on and "sitting with" the perspective of those who are excluded, dehumanized, or devalued for each of these reasons is worthwhile to feel the urgency of the work in cultivating welcoming, safe, and inclusive classrooms for students across the full range of variability.

When we think of inclusivity, it's natural to envision ways to provide access for students who have academic or physical needs. Naturally, there are procedures in place to make sure the buildings and physical spaces are safe. Although this is certainly a key feature of equitable classrooms, the precursor to inclusive instruction and assessment is establishing culture that is safe in ways beyond physical or academic accessibility—one that is *emotionally safe*. We see emotional safety in classrooms that are welcoming, inclusive, where all learners feel heard and are comfortable using their voice, making mistakes, and feel supported by their teacher and their classmates. In a safe environment, we see diversity of all types as a valued and the perspectives of students from the range of variability as a meaningful contribution and a strength.

Students who feel excluded or disliked because of a difference from a majority group may live with these feelings of stress throughout the school day. Even if the feeling isn't as intense as an acute trauma, the slow-burning stress over time takes a toll not only on the ability to learn, but also on a person's health and wellbeing (Suliman et al., 2009). We may notice the exclusion of some of our students, but many students feel sadness, depression, and exclusion without our ever knowing they experience this. Without a sense of belonging and safety, students who feel unwelcomed likely will not feel comfortable enough to express their needs. To create equitable, inclusive classrooms where everyone is embraced, we can't wait until we need to react to an obvious conflict or expressed stress. We have to assume this probability and plan proactively. Establishing a culture that values differences is one that intentionally brings calm to the classroom and a space for all students to participate free from fear of humiliation or teasing.

REFLECTION

What do you think of when you feel that a place or people are "inviting?" How would you describe that setting? Those people? The interactions?

_____

_____

_____

_____

What do you think of when you feel that a place or people are "disinviting?" How would you describe that setting? Those people? The interactions?

_____

_____

_____

_____

BEING INTENTIONALLY INVITING

William Purkey and his colleagues coined the term "Invitational Education" in the 1970s. Their aim was to lead schools to be so intentionally inviting that the both students and families were voluntarily engaged with their school enthusiastically. And they found great success with the practices they honed over many years. Being intentionally inviting is a concept that a district or school can use to improve relationships with families and students, but it's also one we can use to reflect on and strengthen our individual classroom practices. Invitational Education includes the four elements of trust, respect, optimism, and genuine caring (Purkey & Novak, 1996).

ELEMENTS OF INVITATIONS	
Trust	To be inviting, we show students we trust them and we develop students' trust of us by being reliable, consistent, personal, authentic, and honest. Trust can be difficult to gain if students have had a string of poor experiences in school and they've lost their trust in a teacher in the past.
Respect	Invitational classrooms show respect for all students. We do this by holding the belief that all students are valuable human beings and deserve to be treated accordingly.
Optimism	All students are capable of engaging and learning. Invitational classrooms show an expectation of positive, high outcomes for each student.
Caring	We show students that we care through our warmth, empathy, and genuine interest in them.

There are numerous ways every day that we naturally show our students each of the elements above. By becoming *intentional* about these elements within our spaces, content, and the way we teach and interact to invite our students, we create an environment that is not only safe, it's warm and welcoming to each student. Every action we take within the walls of our classrooms can be categorized as intentionally or unintentionally inviting or disinviting.

INTENTIONALITY OF INVITATIONS	
Intentionally Inviting I acted in a way on purpose to enhance the positive outcomes or potential of a person.	**Unintentionally Inviting** I didn't plan to, but I acted in a way that enhanced the positive outcomes or potential of a person.
Intentionally Disinviting I behaved with the intent to disrupt the positive outcomes or potential of a person.	**Unintentionally Disinviting** I accidentally did something that disrupted the positive outcomes or potential of a person.

Because we are human, everyone acts in each of these quadrants at some point in our lives. The goal is to become more inviting and more intentional about being inviting in our classrooms.

ACTION

Consider each of the quadrants of intentionality with invitations. What is an example of each, from either an action that you've seen or one of your own for each quadrant?

INTENTIONALITY OF INVITATIONS	
Intentionally Inviting	**Unintentionally Inviting**
Intentionally Disinviting	**Unintentionally Disinviting**

RELATIONSHIPS THAT VALUE DIVERSITY

Engagement and academic success are not only about the instruction and environment being accessible and interesting or relevant. Rita Pierson in her 2013 TED Talk infamously remarked that "children don't learn from people they don't like." It's also the case that they don't learn from adults they don't think like them. Positive relationships between teacher and student make a significant difference in students' outcomes (student-teacher relationship: $d = .47$). To build student motivation and self-regulation, we have to empower our learners and "share the stage" with them. In this way, teachers take on the roles of mentor and facilitator instead of superior.

STUDENT-TEACHER RELATIONSHIPS

	$d=.47$	
–1.00	0.0	1.50

Stereotype Threat

Unfortunately, there are students who come to school with established biases toward variability in race, ethnicity, gender, socioeconomics, sexual orientation, nationality, ability, or religion. A person experiences stereotype threat when they are on the receiving end of bias in which they perceive they are negatively judged against a societal belief held about a group they're a part of (stereotype threat: $d = -.64$). Negative assumptions about traditionally marginalized, minority groups of people threaten the safety of our classrooms and ability of students to make friends and require our proactive attention. Because these views are usually a mirroring of those held by students' families, teachers are sometimes the only adults in a student's life to teach the value of diversity. Teachers have little to no control over home and local opinions or society at large, but we lead the culture within our classrooms. Teachers bear the responsibility of creating a climate in their classrooms that sends a clear message that discrimination is not accepted and that each student is to be welcomed, celebrated, and made to feel supported by everyone in the classroom.

STEREOTYPE THREAT

d=-.64		
-1.00	0.0	1.50

Ignoring the variability in our students isn't the answer (e.g., being "color blind" or ignoring gender identity). When we ignore differences that are a part of students' identity, it's like saying, "I don't see you," or "I'm uncomfortable with who you are." Ignoring isn't the route to building an inclusive climate. Students notice and mention differences. And teachers aren't blind to variation in skin color. More likely, claiming to be "color blind" is a coping mechanism to avoid the discomfort of existing bias. When teachers ignore differences and aren't proactive in squashing discrimination, micro aggressions can quickly escalate and go down the toxic path of bullying (bullying: $d = -.33$). Zero tolerance of any type of bullying or hate speech is not only our responsibility but also a safety issue. Both the act of bullying and being the victim of bullying are significant risk factors for immediate and future violence (Burgess et al., 2006).

BULLYING

d=-.33		
-1.00	0.0	1.50

Valuing Diversity in Ability

Society as a whole is ableist. This is evident in who we celebrate: those who are the most able, the most successful, in careers we view as prestigious, in athletics, in academics, and on and on. We see this ableism in our schools in the ways we exclude and how we neglect to celebrate diverse skills and accomplishments. This isn't about awarding each student in the same way—the proverbial "everyone gets a trophy"—but rather celebrating authentically the unique ways each student shines. If we really value curiosity, creativity, kindness, empathy, citizenship, and so forth, how are we celebrating this?

Schools also make decisions that exclude and segregate students who have Individualized Education Programs (IEPs). Yes, the very document that is designed to protect the rights of students who are more likely have long-term needs for support, is exactly the document that can serve to marginalize and cause harm to them. We'll think about solutions to this in greater depth in the chapter on service delivery, but we often decide where and by whom students are served based on whether they have an IEP, rather than on what needs individual students have. Hanging on to the false dichotomy of disability plays out in very real ways that discriminate against students with IEPs.

"Can the student meet grade level criteria?" For upper school at least, this question is often the gatekeeper of whether a student is placed in a general education classroom for a course. Said another way, the student's ability in this content area is how we determine if a student *deserves* to be in a class. This may seem harsh, but this is the reality of how students and families often feel when relegated to a special education setting. Given that we have evidence to show that students with IEPs have better outcomes when included in classrooms with students who don't have IEPs (National Council on Disability, 2018), we have a compelling reason to ask a different question. What if instead of asking if the student can perform well enough to pass this class or meet grade level criteria we ask, "What valuable learning can the student gain in this class?"

About a decade ago, my older child, who has dyslexia, needed support with both reading and writing. Mandarin class was offered at his middle school. Now, a surface response could've been, "He can't learn Mandarin at the same level as his peers and isn't likely to meet the expectations of the class, so this isn't the right class for him." But that's not how his school approached it. They knew the value of being in a foreign language class. There was never a discussion of whether he *should* be in the class; the discussion was all around what he could learn in the class. And if you travel to places where the primary language is not one you speak, you know that having an understanding of spoken phrases and words, and immersion in the culture are all incredibly valuable—valuable in even how you see the world (foreign language: $d = .85$). You don't have to meet all the requirements of writing and grammar and spelling of a foreign language course to gain valuable skills and understandings. And you don't have to meet all of these requirements to contribute meaningfully to the group. If we really value the perspectives, contributions, and people of varied abilities, we will embrace this variation in our classrooms and think creatively and with an open mind to *figure out* how to make instruction work for all.

FOREIGN LANGUAGE

d=.85

-1.00   0.0   1.50

Supporting Variation in Gender and Sexual Orientation

In recent years, there has been increasing awareness around gender identity and sexual orientation, and how each of these is neither simple nor dichotomous—again, a false dichotomy. Variation in sexual orientation was the topic of whispered conversations just a few decades ago but is now widely represented in American culture, although often not valued. Increasingly, people see that variation in sexual orientation is as all other types of variability—normal variation with no version more valuable than any other. Variation in gender identity, though, has persisted longer as a category for discrimination, hate, and lack of acceptance. But people who have birth-assigned sex identity that mismatches their gender, those who have fluid gender identity, and those who don't associate their identity with gender, are among the numerous examples of variations in gender identity that have been recorded throughout human history, albeit with varying degrees of acceptance.

Normalizing variation in sexual orientation and gender identity through our words, actions, and representation in classroom content, shows that we value all students and all variations of sexual orientation and gender identity. Because so often the default is *no* representation or an ignoring of these topics, students who don't fit the majority categories are essentially invalidated. And their perspectives are never heard. People are not heard. Thus, an intentional validation can have an enormous protective effect for the student who feels alone.

There is no room for discussion or wavering in universally designed classrooms: using a student's chosen name and pronouns is the only option in a classroom designed to nurture the physical and emotional well-being of all students. Teachers' sharing their own pronouns sends a message that variability in gender identity is normal and valued. Giving students the opportunity to privately share their own preferences for pronouns in the classroom allows for intentional affirmation of students. According to The Trevor Project's National Survey on LGTBQIA Youth Mental Health, their national study showed that LGTBQIA youth with at least one affirming adult confidant were 40% less likely to attempt suicide than those had none (Trevor Project, 2021). Acceptance of students of the LGTBQIA community and their identities saves lives. Talk about making a difference! Validation in this way actually saves lives.

There are many schools throughout the country, particularly in rural areas, that have policies against speaking about sexual orientation and gender—or at least speaking about the minority populations within each. There do not seem to be policies against heteronormative or cisgender references. No doubt, history will not be kind to these discriminatory policies any more than history is forgiving to policies and practices of racial segregation from a few short decades ago. Many of you may find yourselves in teaching or leadership positions in such schools, often within less inclusive communities. Many of us have at one time or another walked the balance between staying employed and pushing the system to do the "right thing." By choosing this book, you likely are wanting to be as inclusive and accommodating as you can. While it isn't the intent of this book to suggest you break policies of your school (we certainly need as many inclusive educators as possible employed in our schools), we can all find ways to be validating to all of humans in our care, in both subtle and overt ways. To do so is absolutely the right thing to do.

Valuing People and Perspectives of Varied Racial Backgrounds

It certainly is no secret that racism is alive and well in the United States, and as we've seen play out in the media time and again, there is no one region of the country that has exclusive ownership of this blight. Each educator has the ever-present job of implementing and improving upon anti-racist efforts in the classroom. All teachers have to actively send messages, overt and embedded, that diversity in race is a strength. The perspective that each student brings to the table creates space for everyone in the group to learn and grow, when facilitated skillfully in a safe environment. The world may not be safe for people of all racial backgrounds and make ups, but we can certainly lead and teach differently and intentionally within our classrooms.

There are many scholars who lead deep professional learning in education on racial equity. Glenn Singleton's work on Courageous Conversations is an excellent example. Racism in schools has its own ability to harm beyond what we see in our society at large. In addition to the cumulative trauma BIPOC young people experience at school and in the community, educational practices themselves often inflict harm, further depressing the likelihood of academic success.

Perhaps because of being raised in Selma, Alabama in the 1970s and 1980s, race and racism are topics that have been on my mind for as long as I can remember. Although Selma holds a historical place in the Civil Rights Movement, progress toward inclusion and nonviolent communication in Selma seems to have lagged far behind towns of similar size in other parts of the country. I didn't fully understand the major racial divide that ripped through Selma's public high school in the 1989–1990 academic year. Although it was happening to my school during my junior year, I didn't really try to understand. Now as an educator, educational researcher, and adult, I see what happened as pivotal and a reflection of a practice that continues to persist in pockets of our country.

The school superintendent at the time launched an aggressive fight against "tracking" practices in the public school system. He saw that racial inequities in instructional grouping practices resulted in poor outcomes for Black students. In those days, the youngest learners were "tracked" in Kindergarten and first grade into groups based on their performance: low, middle, and high, especially for reading. Presumably, the groupings allowed teachers to move forward with students who had already mastered the content, while allowing more time for students who were behind. But the students in the lower groups didn't receive the same core instruction with supplemental instruction or intervention to improve; they received slower-paced instruction as a replacement for the core instruction.

The superintendent understood that this tracking into the low group without access to the higher, core instruction was an educational death sentence. Those students never moved out of the low group. Instead, they sank further and further behind as the clock ticked loudly and days, months, and years accumulated. Although there were small performance differences among students in these groups in early grades, tracking led to a dismal trajectory of growth for those students in the low group, leaving most unable to read in high school. And who was tracked into the low group? Mostly Black students.

In grade nine, the "high" group became Level I, the "middle" group Level II, and "low" group Level III. Worse, this access continued to be divided sharply along racial lines. By high school, the Level III students performed many grades behind on critical literacy, problem-solving, and mathematics skills. They had a poor chance at career readiness, no chance at college readiness, and a far lower likelihood of high school graduation. Those students weren't less capable of learning—the system had failed to teach them. Students gave up because systemic racism told them they can't achieve or access the same education and success as their white counterparts.

This narrative is not unique to Selma. The statistics for Black students are revealed in large studies in our country:

> *Black students are less likely than White students to have access to college-ready courses. Only 57 percent of Black students have access to a full range of math and science courses necessary for college readiness, compared to with 81 percent of Asian American students and 71 percent of white students. (US Department of Education, Office of Civil Rights, 2014)*

Even when Black students do have access to honors or advanced placement courses, they are vastly under-represented in these courses. Black and Latino students represent 38 percent of students in schools that offer AP courses, but only 29 percent of students enrolled in at least one AP course. Black and Latino students also have less access to gifted and talented education programs than white students. (US Department of Education, Office of Civil Rights, 2014)

Research has shown evidence of systematic bias in teacher expectations for Black students. Non-Black teachers were found to have lower expectations of Black students than Black teachers. (Gershenson et al., 2015)

Students of color are often concentrated in schools with fewer resources with less qualified teachers, teachers with lower salaries and novice teachers. (Amerikaner, 2012)

Black boys are disproportionally labeled as having behavior disorders. (National Center for Learning Disabilities, 2020)

Black boys are likely to receive harsher punishment for the same behavior as their White counterparts. (National Center for Learning Disabilities, 2020)

When a largely white, female workforce is not well versed in culturally responsive teaching and concepts such as high- and low-context cultures, mislabeling of behaviors that are outside of a teacher's norms is common. Once labeled, Black boys are more often placed in separate special education rooms where they remain until they graduate or, more often, until they drop out of school (Lewis, 1998). I wonder where those 50-year-old former Level III students from Selma High School are today. How many are in poverty today? How many were denied the ability to learn skills needed to be employed? Today, Selma has a startling profile of violence. How many of those once-energetic kindergartners have become a part of that statistic because they were failed by the educational system? Then I think, "What could they have been if in Kindergarten they had access to the same core instruction as the white students?"

How many who only needed someone to teach them to read would be professors, physicians, attorneys, politicians, or business owners? The answers to these questions should break our hearts. The answers should compel us to act and talk courageously, and with urgency.

REFLECTION

What are the ways your school or you ensure that students from minority populations feel valued, are heard, and are protected? Where do you see there are gaps? What examples do you have of a student or students from a minority group in your school being excluded, undervalued, or otherwise harmed?

_____

_____

_____

_____

_____

INTENTIONALLY TEACH INCLUSION AND EQUITY

The examples above are the most prevalent categories in which students not in the majority are excluded and at risk for harm. Policies, practices, and procedures perpetuate this exclusion and reflect the discrimination we see in society as a whole. To create a safe environment for our students, we have to be aware of these biases in the institutions in which we work, and in ourselves. Beyond these most common categories of exclusion are religion, nationality, language, sex, and SES. Each of these is worthy of our reflection and action as we create safe learning spaces that represent diversity prominently in content, perspectives, photos in every corner of the school.

CASE STORY

As Ms. Talbert began planning for the upcoming year, she wanted to make some changes to the first units of the year to create a culture and climate of equity and inclusion in her class. She didn't only want all students to be *accepting* of diversity; she wanted all students to *value* diversity! She reviewed the readings she had planned for the early units and selected new ones so that diversity was represented—and not in a token way, but rather was truly the ethos of her classroom. She was intentional to bring in perspectives that spanned diversity in race, gender identity, sexual orientation, language, ability, nationality, and so forth. And she purposefully thought about the order in which perspectives were given so that white, cisgender, heterosexual, male, highly able perspectives were not presented first or featured more prominently.

Ms. Talbert decided that while these decisions with regard to diversity within her lessons was a positive change, that she wanted to be more explicit in teaching her students the value of diversity, equity, inclusion, and social justice in her classroom. In her first lesson, Ms. Talbert introduced her students to the concept of diversity in opinion and perspective. Her intention was for students to see that when there is no diversity, there is stagnation, a lack of growth. She wanted her students to know what she knew: diversity is our strength. But society does not favor diversity and assigns power accordingly. She set up six stations around her room with videos, primary source readings, competing headlines in the media, and photographs to illustrate these ideas. Students made choices about where to engage and moved through three rotations each. Following the rotations in which students interacted with one another, Ms. Talbert asked students to reflect quietly and summarize in writing or with illustration their thoughts about the value of diversity in society and challenges to solve. She invited students to share their reflections with the group, but did not require anyone to do so. She took notes about the spoken reflections, and collected the written and illustrated ones.

Ms. Talbert closed the loop in this lesson by explicitly talking about how diversity in race, gender identity, sexual orientation, nationality, language, and intellectual differences were valued in her class. While the world is not always kind to smaller

(Continued)

(Continued)

groups or those who have traditionally not been in power, this would not be the case in her classroom. She told her students that her classroom was a safe space where all students were heard and that she would interrupt any "unsafe" words or expression within the class.

Ms. Talbert then shared a bit about herself, including her preferred pronouns (she/her), and invited students to write a profile of their strengths, goals for the year, and anything they'd like for her to know about themselves, including the pronouns they'd like for her to use. She went to a table removed from the group and asked students who would prefer to talk about themselves instead of writing to visit her one at a time at the table.

This wasn't the end of Ms. Talbert's explicit instruction on diversity. It was a theme she intended to give attention to in each unit throughout the year.

PROTECT EACH STUDENT'S VOICE

Emotionally safe classrooms go beyond representation of minority populations, although this is certainly foundational. Classroom teachers facilitate growth by leading the interaction and functioning of groups of students. Teachers can easily put into place norms of collaboration to establish a safer learning environment in which each student's voice is protected from harm by other students, and the culture of the classroom is a collaborative, not competitive, one.

There are plenty of natural moments to guide students in respectful discussions about differences and acceptance. Safe environments teach and model peaceful conflict resolution and prepare students to be effective advocates for themselves and others. Teachers provide opportunities for students to work together and socialize with one another. They provide language for discussing feelings and helping students learn to communicate with one another and accept constructive criticism. When conflicts arise, teachers guide students through safe conflict resolution strategies and always foster an atmosphere of respect and inclusivity.

Groups that establish norms of collaboration function better and protect the voices of each member of the group (Garmston & Wellman, 2016). Norms of collaboration work best when they are generated by the group, rather than imposed upon them. Offering norms for the group to revise and add to can be a great way to engage students in this process. It then becomes the role of the full group, not only the teacher, to guide the group back to the norms as needed, in respectful ways.

CASE STORY

Ms. Talbert guided her class to establish norms of collaboration for the year. She started with the norms of "(I) Everyone's voice is valuable, (2) Presume positive intent in others, and (3) Disagree respectfully." She led the group in conversation, and they arrived at the following norms:

I.   Everyone's voice is valuable, and everyone gets a turn.

2.   Presume positive intent of everyone.

3.   We can disagree, but we do so without yelling, calling names, rolling eyes, or anything else that is seen as disrespectful.

4.   We take turns talking and do not talk over anyone.

5.   We try to see each other's points of view.

6.   We pay attention to others and ask questions to make sure we understand what they are saying.

TEACH SELF-REGULATION

Self-regulation includes all the skills we use to manage and organize our thoughts and emotions and use this information to guide our actions (Zimmerman, 2001). Think about the last time you felt threatened in some way. Or you felt an intense emotion of stress or sadness. Recall the details of that event and what was giving you the emotion. As you think about this, where do you notice that feeling in your body under these times of distress? Maybe you feel a lump in your throat. Or perhaps it's a tightening in your chest. You could feel queasy in your stomach or have a headache. It's pretty uncomfortable to imagine sitting with those feelings for very long, isn't it? Can you imagine trying to learn something new while experiencing this stress? The thought probably seems impossible. Dysregulation itself, then, is a barrier to accessing instruction.

SELF-REGULATION

d = .54

-1.00   0.0   1.50

When students dysregulate and behave in an unexpected way that is either harmful to themselves or to others, it often feels like that moment, during the unexpected behavior, is the time to intervene and suggest how the student should've made a different choice or to outline an immediate consequence to take away a likely reinforcer of the behavior. This is often the approach advocated within applied behavior analysis. Although this may work in the short term to decrease a behavior, this alone does not teach regulation. In other words, this may make the teacher's life better, but it may not actually help the student.

In the moments when we experience a strong emotion, we are not thinking with the logical part of our brain. The mental energy is diverted to the part of our brain responsible for emotions. When this happens, we are unable to think as logically until the emotion is deescalated and the energy returns to the logical center of our brain. All this to say, when a student is experiencing an intense emotion, this is not the time to correct. It is time to connect. Think of an "out to lunch" sign on the student's forehead. Their logical brain is unavailable in that moment. Instead, by identifying and validating a student's emotions, we can then return to discuss that emotion and the strategies for learning to regulate when feeling that emotion in the future. Rather than punishing the student in a way that isn't connected to the emotion, we guide the student to repair the harm and regulate in the future. Dominique Smith's work on Restorative Practices is an excellent resource for deep understanding of this type of support.

Self-regulation also includes the ways we use our mental processes to manage tasks and develop skills for learning. Self-regulated learners continuously monitor their own progress toward goals and make changes to their efforts and actions in response to their progress (Berk, 2003). We see self-regulation in our students when they aren't depending on a teacher to tell them how they are doing—they understand the learning intentions and success criteria, they have a clear sense of their own progress, and then they make decisions about how to improve. Self-regulated learners are aware of their own thought processes and have identified the strategies that help them learn best (self-regulation: $d = .54$).

Self-regulation is not something students have or don't have—it is something we develop over time, and some of us need targeted instruction to gain. Teaching self-regulation in the classroom is something we have to do explicitly and within all of the lessons and learning experiences we facilitate. This involves guiding students to set their own goals, giving them a turn to reflect on their performance before imposing our feedback, and giving students lots of learning strategies and then guiding them to figure out which strategies work best for their learning.

CASE STORY

Ms. Talbert noticed that Charlene seemed particularly anxious when there was a large-group discussion. Ms. Talbert never required or even prompted particular students to speak in front of the group, but Charlene was still visibly nervous during these times of the day.

Ms. Talbert asked Charlene to visit her during a planning period so she could have a private conversation with her about the anxiety. Charlene had been pretty open with Ms. Talbert in the past about the times she feels most anxious.

Ms. Talbert asked Charlene about what she'd noticed, "I'm getting the sense that you may be uncomfortable during our whole-group discussions. Is that what you're feeling?" Charlene responded, "Yeah. I'm not sure why, but I feel really antsy." Ms. Talbert reminded Charlene that she never expected anyone to speak out loud, and Charlene affirmed, "I know."

(Continued)

(Continued)

Ms. Talbert invited Charlene to journal about the feelings she was having as soon after the group experience as she can. Counselors Ms. Talbert had worked with in the past suggested this, as a great strategy to use with all students.

"Once you journal about this a bit, we can talk about what you discover and see if we can come up with some strategies to help. I can ask Mr. Martinez to help us brainstorm, too, if you like." Charlene agreed this all seemed like a good idea.

After, Ms. Talbert checked in to see if Charlene had a chance to journal and had any ideas about the anxiety she was feeling. Ms. Talbert was pretty sure she was feeling anxious because she had started sitting at the front of the room. That's the only change she could identify. But she held back with this suggestion to give Charlene a chance to use metacognitive skills to develop self-regulation.

Charlene responded to Ms. Talbert's check in, "You know, when I thought more about my feelings and what's making them happen, I think it's because I feel like everyone's looking at me. And because they are all behind me, that makes it worse." Before making the suggestion that Charlene move to the back, she asked, "What about everyone looking at you makes you feel anxious?" Charlene thought for a few seconds and said, "I guess I think they're laughing at me or judging me."

Ms. Talbert paused for a few seconds and asked, "What do you think might help make your anxiety better?" Charlene affirmed that moving to the back of the room would help, but she also added, "I think it might help to remind myself in the moment that they aren't really laughing at me or judging me. And if anyone is, it's not really a big deal."

Ms. Talbert smiled, "That sounds like a great idea, Charlene!" "How do you think you can remind yourself to give yourself that affirmation?" "I don't know," "Charlene said after thinking for a bit."

Then, Ms. Talbert offered some suggestions, "Well, maybe a picture, or a word, or even an acronym could help. Or counting to 10 and breathing slowly. What do you think about one of those?"

Charlene thought that was a good idea and said she'd think about the best one to use. The next day, Charlene made eye contact with Ms. Talbert and tapped a picture she'd drawn and taped to the inside cover of her notebook. It was a picture of an eye, with the number "10" in the pupil.

Ms. Talbert felt great that with a few questions, Charlene was able to figure out what worked for herself in that situation. She knew that Charlene would be able to figure strategies for other situations with this developing self-regulation skill.

MANAGING STRESS

Managing stress is a skill we would all probably say we could benefit from improving. An inability to manage stress is more than uncomfortable; it impacts our health. In emotionally safe classrooms, like Ms. Talbert's, we intentionally teach students to manage and regulate stress of all sources, such as interpersonal relationships, home life, discrimination and "isms," exclusion, workload or work level, and overwhelming emotions. Ms. Talbert coached Charlene through this discovery, rather than immediately offering her own suggestions. In emotionally safe classrooms, teachers guide students to manage stress through mindfulness exercises such as breathing, counting, meditating, and visualizing (mindfulness: $d = .28$).

MINDFULNESS

$d = .28$		

–1.00   0.0   1.50

To take charge over managing their own stress as they develop skills, we can point students to apps that teach and guide mindfulness. Rather than limiting breaks to teacher-determined times, teachers can give students the autonomy to take breaks when they are feeling intense stress. We can encourage students, in the way Charlene was, to journal about their feelings of readiness and to advocate for themselves when they need help. Classrooms designed to support all students are focused on more than behavior and task completion—they are designed to develop expert learners, resilient to, and managers of their own emotions and stresses. To accomplish this, we have to talk about emotions and stresses and provide a wealth of strategies for students to try until they find the right ones for them.

REFLECTION

Think for a moment about the last conversation you heard about a difficult student challenge, perhaps in a teachers' lounge. Did the words demonstrate a trust of the student? Was it respectful? Did it show optimism for the

(Continued)

(Continued)

student? Was it empathic and caring? How could that conversation be "rewritten" to include more of the elements of invitation?

_____

_____

_____

_____

_____

 **ACTION**

In what specific ways can we explicitly value diversity? Following are a few of the many examples of ways we can show students we value diversity and, thus, value each one of them. Which of these do you unintentionally do? Which do you do with intention? Which do you aim to use with intention in the future? What would you add to this list that you either use or have as a priority to use?

EXAMPLE STRATEGIES
☐ Use a student's chosen name and pronouns.
☐ Refrain from asking any student to "speak for" a group of which they are a part.
☐ Give students options to participate rather than valuing large-group speaking as best.
☐ Offer your own pronouns and welcome (but not require) all students to share theirs.

EXAMPLE STRATEGIES

☐ Give feedback on behavior privately rather than publicly.

☐ Represent in text, spoken words, content, and images people who span variability in race, gender, sexual orientation, ability, religion, and nationality.

☐ Place a "safe space" sign in your room to indicate your valuing of LGBTQIA+ students and willingness to listen or offer support.

☐ Accurately depict historical and current events using unbiased sources.

☐ Celebrate holidays and traditions that span cultures, religions, and nationalities.

☐ Lead the group of students to establish norms for their collaboration.

☐ Give students the chance to revise their work and grow before assigning a grade.

☐ Advocate for a group that you are not a part of that has been marginalized.

☐ Acknowledge and validate that those in minority groups of every category of variation have been and continue to experience discrimination and hate by those in majority groups.

☐ Intentionally balance participation in ways that value everyone's voice but don't value extraversion.

☐ Validate student's intense emotions before offering a correction.

☐ Give students strategies, time, and space to manage relative degrees of stress.

☐ Actively address bias, discrimination, exclusion, and bullying in your teaching content.

☐ Use warm facial expressions and eye contact.

☐ Individually greet and acknowledge students with warmth.

(Continued)

(Continued)

EXAMPLE STRATEGIES

☐ Demonstrate authenticity and show your "humanity" to your students.

☐ Show empathy and support to students.

☐ Ensure each student knows you believe they can succeed.

☐ Minimize public displays that compare performance or behaviors.

☐ Use small groups, where taking risks may feel safer.

☐ Use assessments that provide anonymity or avoid public display.

☐ Give students the option to work in small groups or alone.

☐ Ensure "participation" includes options other than speaking in a large group.

☐ Vary between individual reflection and collaborative learning.

☐ Use "no hands up" think time before inviting contributions from the whole group.

☐ Use a talking stick.

☐ Assign roles of "talker" and "questioners." Rotate roles.

Others. . .

☐

☐

☐

☐

SUMMARY

We need to rewrite the narrative for the students who are vulnerable in our schools. Give each student a voice and protect their voice. Show each one the potential you see for contribution and leadership and channel their engagement it in positive ways. You can be the impetus for resilience desperately needed in a world that continues to tell people, "You are less valuable because of..." your skin color, your gender identity, your sexual orientation, your ability, the language you speak, your religion, your sex, where you were born, how much money your family has, or any other category the societies of the world use to exclude and harm. We cannot protect our students from experiencing harm and "isms" in the world, but we can provide a safe space, give them a voice, and teach them strategies to self-regulate and manage stress. By doing so, we play a small part in preparing them to take these life-long challenges "head on" and thrive in the face of that reality.

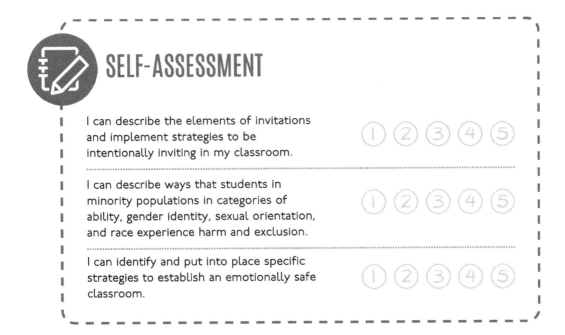

SELF-ASSESSMENT

I can describe the elements of invitations and implement strategies to be intentionally inviting in my classroom.	① ② ③ ④ ⑤
I can describe ways that students in minority populations in categories of ability, gender identity, sexual orientation, and race experience harm and exclusion.	① ② ③ ④ ⑤
I can identify and put into place specific strategies to establish an emotionally safe classroom.	① ② ③ ④ ⑤

CHAPTER THREE

Options for Expression

By Giving Students Options to Express Their Learning, We Reduce Inequities in Assessment

MR. BARTON FOUND HIS STUDENTS KNEW MORE THAN HE THOUGHT WHEN HE GAVE THEM OPTIONS TO SHOW THEIR LEARNING.

Learning Intensions	Success Criteria
I am learning about the difference between tasks versus skills and understandings.	I can argue the importance of a focus on skills and understanding instead of tasks.
I am learning about confounding variables in assessment.	I can identify potential confounding variables in my assessments and describe how those are barriers for students.
I am learning about options for expression.	I can map a skill or understanding from a standard to many tasks in which a student can show their skill or understanding.

Take a moment to think about your favorite teacher and all you learned from that person, all that person gave you. Maybe that teacher taught you to believe in yourself, or to be kinder, or captured your interest for content in a new way. No doubt, you connected to this teacher, and you felt this teacher cared about you. Perhaps this person was incredibly skilled at teaching you content that was really difficult for you and gave you a new way of thinking. Many of the most important gems you gained from that teacher were never even assessed. Your learning experience with this teacher was broad, and rich, and complex and could never fully be captured in the classroom assessments you completed, nor should it have been. We would spend all of our time assessing if we tried to capture via assessments *everything* we taught!

MAKING CHOICES ABOUT PRIORITIES

In order to plan for the most meaningful, and yet the most efficient, classroom assessments, we have to first gain consensus on the *purpose* of our classroom assessments—and what is beyond their scope. The aim of our day-to-day classroom assessments is not to understand and document with a broad brush *all* that a student has gained, but rather to know precisely where a student is toward specific, selected targets in order to guide a student's next steps and plan instruction. We also use classroom assessment to determine when students' need additional support or intervention or further diagnostic assessment. Classroom assessment is how we pinpoint strengths and needs and the effectiveness of our instruction to gage what changes we need to make to support students to continue on the path toward some goal. A view of assessment as a planning tool, rather than an endpoint, requires that we go deep with our assessments and use what we learn from them. But because it's not possible to assess deeply everything we teach, we must prioritize our targets to determine what we assess by asking what matters *most*. What we value as most important can't always be found in the academic standards. When we think about what we learned in school (or wish we'd learned in school!), the priorities are often skills like studying, organization, communication, collaboration, creativity, problem-solving, conflict resolution, strong executive functioning and regulation, and the like. Taking a bigger picture view of our lessons and units and what we value most—what our portrait of a graduate is—we see opportunities and a responsibility to teach and assess beyond the academic standards.

Because we want to maximize our time in instruction and, thus, our efficiency in assessment, it's always important that we choose which of these skills and understandings matter most. Prioritizing becomes even more important when we are teaching online, because we don't have large blocks of time with students in the same classroom. Teaching during the pandemic, we were forced to measure only what mattered most, and in many ways this offered an important (and liberating!) lesson: we don't have to constantly assess every standard or everything we teach. Your favorite teacher you were just thinking about taught you essential skills or understandings plus a lot of otherwise life-enhancing skills or understandings. When it comes time for assessment, we want to focus our efforts on the essential skills and understandings. And what makes a skill or understanding essential? An essential skill or understanding is one that the student will need for a lifetime.

At first glance, it may seem to make sense to ask what subjects matter the most, but this approach is artificially compartmentalized and doesn't lead to answers that work for every student. Consider, for example, the student for whom art will be the foundation of their career. For this student, art may have been seen as "extra" or "enriching" or an elective, rather than foundational, possibly most important subject that student takes. What's most important for any given student depends on the path they take later in life and can rarely be predicted. Instead of going the route of judging the relative merit of *subjects,* we should instead take on the task of prioritizing *skills and understandings*. What we need to select are those skills and understandings that are life changing—the skills that keep the most doors open for our students as they choose their career paths and become adult citizens in their communities.

 ACTION

As a small team with your colleagues, have each person reflect and write down one idea per card or post-it-note a skill or understanding that is essential for students to have for life or to keep doors open. You might start with a prompt of having everyone to think about the most important skills and understandings they gained in school—or *wish* they'd gained in school. Continue until each person has contributed 4–6 ideas.

Next, take all of the cards or post-it-notes, and group them into themes of similar skills and understandings. How many themes did you generate? What do you notice about the themes?

Finally, in small groups or pairs (if this was completed with more than 10 people), each person considers an assessment you have conducted recently. Were any of the themes the group identified present in your assessment? Were any of these the primary focus? Would you or would you not revise the assessment based on this discussion? If so, what would you do differently?

SKILLS AND UNDERSTANDINGS VERSUS TASKS

Early in my career, I spent a lot of time assessing young children's development using standardized instruments. With one of those instruments, the Battelle Developmental Inventory, one of the items was to prompt the child to stack nine, one-inch cubes in a coffee cup. But stacking the blocks in the coffee cup isn't the important *skill*—it's only the task. You can go your entire life and *never* stack nine, one-inch cubes in a coffee cup and be just fine. In fact, you probably have gone your whole life without doing this, unless you've administered a Battelle. So, why is it that this item is on the test? It turns out, this item is one way we can look at a number of skills that a child has. We can see what type of grasp they use to pick up the block, we can see if they seem to have spatial matching skills, and we can see (probably most importantly), if they persist at a difficult task, even if they initially fail. These are all important skills! The block stacking is just a measure; it's only the task. And it isn't the most interesting task, so on more than one occasion, even with all of my best toddler engagement tricks, I was unable to get the child interested in the blocks and the coffee cup. Did this mean the child did not have a radial-digital grasp, spatial matching, and mastery motivation? Not at all! And we could look for evidence of those skills as the child interacted with other toys and items during their play. There are many tasks to see evidence of any skill. And the same is true for all that we teach preschool through college. There are tasks designed to measure skills, but every single time, the skills and understandings are what matter; the tasks are only the measure.

Improving the quality of our assessments requires that we have a clear understanding of the difference between *skills/understandings* and *tasks*. In a mastery learning environment, our focus is on improving skills and understandings that go far beyond the walls of a classroom, or an assignment, and extend beyond the years a student spends in their academic years.

When my older child was in high school chemistry class, the students were to memorize the first two rows of the periodic table of elements. This was the big assessment of one of the units. I'm sure if we were to ask any practicing chemist what the most important skills or understandings a person needs in life relative to chemistry or even what the most important skills or understandings a student needs in order to keep doors open for a career in science, memorizing the first two rows of the periodic table of elements wouldn't even make the top 25 list. Memorizing the elements was only a *task*. What we need to identify is the *skill or understanding* that is important so we can determine what our options are for the tasks to measure. Having only a single option for students to show their learning introduces significant inequities and, thus, threats to the validity of our assessments.

MEASURING WHAT WE INTEND TO MEASURE

Once we have identified what the most important skills and understandings it is for students to learn, and, thus, for us to assess, our next task is to ensure that our assessments are measuring these, and that nothing else is getting in the way. That is, if we determine that what's *really* important about this unit in social studies is that students have a deep understanding of different versions of capitalism and the impacts on the wealth divide, then we want to make sure that's exactly what we are measuring—students' deep understanding of this concept.

With clarity on the priorities in hand, teachers can much more easily make decisions about the options to give their students to express their skill/content mastery. If the answer to the question, "When my students truly understand the concept of economic supply and demand when they can explain it using novel examples." It doesn't matter if the students do this in a 1:1 conversation with you, in writing, or in a slide presentation created on the computer. They can choose the method. The clarity prevents old thinking patterns where students must express their understanding in an essay on an assessment.

When we focus on skills and understandings, students are free to use their own talents and preferences to show their learning.

Once teachers are clear on the "vitals" it is our responsibility to share what those skills and understandings are with our students. Students should be made aware of the content for which they are accountable and exactly how you *and they* will know that they have achieved mastery. Teachers and students can work together to discuss their best next steps toward mastery and set goals.

CONFOUNDING VARIABLES

As a professional in the field of education, your teaching is likely evaluated on a regular basis by someone in a leadership or mentorship role. Take a minute to think about how that evaluation looks. Perhaps someone has a reflective conversation with you about your teaching and in some way examines the outcomes of your teaching with your students. Certainly, no evaluation would be complete without an observation of your actual teaching. There are many options for how this observation of your teaching could be carried out. The observation could be scheduled ahead with your input or completely unannounced. There could be only one person observing or several observers. The observation could be a recording of yourself that you select, or it could be live. You could be teaching a lesson you've taught many times, or one you teach for the first time. Your reflection could include a formally written contribution you make, or it could instead be only informal conversation.

As you think about these options for evaluation, are there some options that make you feel more comfortable? Are there some options that make you feel uncomfortable? Are there options that would affect your performance? Now, imagine that your principal or superintendent has asked you to teach live, in front of the full faculty and parents of the school or district on a stage with a spotlight on you. If that sounds comfortable to you, imagine instead that you are teaching on live television and millions of people are watching and interacting online about your performance. What if you were given a timed, multiple-choice test about teaching as your evaluation? Would any of these ways of demonstrating your skills and understanding help you perform better, have no effect, or could this cause you to perform worse?

REFLECTION

How do you perform best? If you are being evaluated in your area of expertise, consider showing what you know in each of the following ways. Rank your performance from most preferred to least preferred with these options. Then, circle any option that would negatively affect your performance—any option that you might not be able to show what you know best.

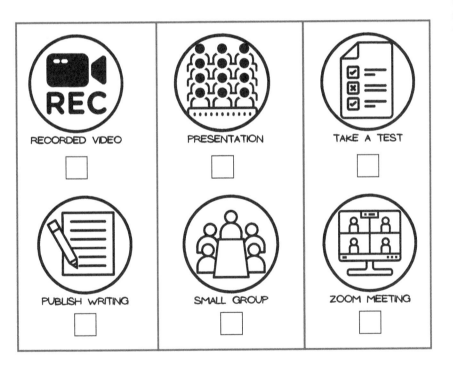

If you perform worse as a teacher in teaching in front of a live audience or on national television, what does this mean about your skills as a teacher? If a student performs poorly on a test, what do we know, and what do we not know, about that student's skills in what we are trying to measure?

Perhaps your performance would be unaffected by any of these conditions. If so, lucky you! But for most of us, one or more of these could actually cause us to perform at a lower level that we normally would. The actual task does impact how we perform. Maybe for you it was the unannounced observation, the performance in front of many people, the formal writing, or the timed test. Or maybe the timed test or formal written response is exactly how you would perform best, but informal conversation would affect your performance.

We don't want the way our classroom assessments are constructed to get in the way of what we are measuring. But so often, that's exactly what happens. "A confounding variable is a variable, other than the independent variable that you're interested in, that may affect the dependent variable. This can lead to erroneous conclusions about the relationship between the independent and dependent variables" (McDonald, 2014, p. 24). In other words, when you are trying to measure the effects of your teaching on student learning, a confounding variable is something other than teaching or student learning that is affecting students' performance on the assessment. That third variable is often the assessment task itself.

I've spent my career in the area of inclusion and intervention; yet, if you asked me to teach others by teaching on national television, I would be incredibly nervous and probably seem as though I don't have a lot of skill in the area. And if what you were trying to measure was my skills in inclusion, the task of teaching on national television for me would be a *confounding variable*. My ability to teach on television isn't what you were trying to measure, but because it impacts my performance, it *is* what you measure. During the pandemic, I learned that I perform better on live video than in recorded video. Perhaps you learned the same, or the opposite, about yourself during our time at home. Regardless, even though our actual knowledge and skills haven't changed, the task does impact our performance. The same is true for our students. If we give every student the same task, for some students, the task itself will introduce a confounding variable.

A few years ago, my daughter started college and enrolled in statistics her first semester. She had taken statistics in high school and felt good about her base of understanding in the subject. Her college professor was a good teacher, using many ways to engage her students and connecting much of the content to real-world applications. My daughter was engaged and learned a lot from the lectures, and almost all the students who attended class regularly seemed to understand the concepts. But many of the students had to drop the class because they were failing. The teacher seemed proud of the low pass rate, presumably because this failure implied rigor.

Before we go further into confounding variables, let's address this issue of rigor. Far too many teachers, mostly at the high school and postsecondary levels, judge the rigor of their courses by the grades students earn in their courses. Make no mistake; rigor is only the bar we set. The grades in a course are largely a reflection of the quality of teaching and assessment. With excellent teaching and assessment practices, there is no limit to the number of students who excel, even in extremely rigorous courses—courses with a high bar. The best teachers set a high bar and get every student there. This is what mastery learning is all about—students working to improve with as many chances as they need with the expectation that they will all get there. And mastery learning has the potential to significantly accelerate students' learning (mastery learning: $d = .61$).

MASTERY LEARNING

$d = .61$

-1.00   0.0   1.50

Any teacher can set a high bar and then not implement quality practices to support students to achieve. A poor pass rate or low average grade is not validation of a rigorous course but instead of poor teaching or assessment.

Why were half of the students in my daughter's statistics class failing if the instruction was so good? Well, in this case, it wasn't the fault of the teaching but instead the assessment practices. Each week in their assessment, students sat at individual computers and completed tasks in which they were required to recall from memory Excel spreadsheet formulae to carry out the statistical procedures and make decisions from the results. I'm sure if we were to ask statisticians to list the most important skills and understandings freshmen students need to keep doors open or for their everyday lives down the road, there would be no emerging theme of memorizing Excel spreadsheet formulae. In fact, probably not a single statistician would have this listed as essential. For the students who had difficulty memorizing the formulae, the tasks that required this skill was a confounding variable to measure their learning on the skills and understandings that were truly essential.

Confounding variables are inherent when we offer only one option to students for action and expression. The confounder swings the advantage to those who prefer or are better at expressing themselves in the required way. To be clear, the advantage is not because the student has a higher skill or deeper understanding on what you are measuring. They simply are better at that mode of showing what they know. And our assessments will continue to be fraught with inequities as long as we don't identify the confounding variables and work intentionally to reduce them through the options we give students.

 ACTION

If our assessments are to serve their intended purpose of informing our instruction by measuring what students can do and understand on what matters most, we have to identify and control for the confounding variables. The first step is to take a look at the way you've decided to assess and determine what the potential confounding variables are for your students. Although you may have your current students in mind as you do this, because all classrooms have variability, the confounding variables you identify for the class you have now will likely apply to many other students you teach in the future.

Consider an upcoming unit and the way you have traditionally measured what students learned as a result of this unit. What is most essential for students to know, be able to do, and understand from this unit? Describe the tasks you usually use to assess student learning. Identify the possible confounding variables for each task.

UNIT:	
Learning Intentions	**Success Criteria**
Assessment Tasks Planned	**Potential Confounding Variables**

CHOOSING OPTIONS FOR EXPRESSION

We all have preferences and conditions under which we perform best, and our students are no different from us. For any given skill or understanding, there are countless ways that we can measure students' learning. But all too often, there is a single, teacher-designed assessment, and options for accommodations come only to students who have an IEP (Individualized Education Program) or 504 plan. The premise is that a standardized assessment makes for a fairer assessment, a more valid one, when, in fact, the opposite is true: giving a single option for showing learning is weighted toward those who have strengths in that option. Some of our students are talented presenters but do not have confidence as "test takers." Some instead find tests easy but are afraid of speaking in front of the class. Some have strengths with writing or graphic design. For many, the idea of something being timed gives a great deal of stress and interferes with their ability to show their learning. Clearly, a student does not have to have a label or IEP for this to be true. In fact, as many students are affected by confounding variables who *don't* have an IEP as there are who do have an IEP.

This variability in performance under certain conditions affects our ability to see what students understand and can do if we only use a single type of assessment. For example, if the only option we give is a timed test, then those students who have test anxiety or need more time for processing are unable to show what they know well. In other words, the validity of the test is compromised *because* we didn't offer another option. It is less fair *because* the assessment is standardized. Ironic, isn't it? In our attempt to be completely fair by keeping the requirements the same, we created an inequity. And here is where the phrase, "fair is not equal," becomes relevant. Imagine how much better students can perform if they have choice in how they show their learning, and barriers, such as timed experiences, are removed. I'm in no way suggesting that students have options for the level of proficiency they show, only in the *way* they show it. We can have the same expectations for skills and understanding in a class presentation as we do in an online video presentation or a paper. Or the same expectations in a test or an oral conference with a teacher.

At first glance, some of the options for expressing learning may seem familiar as they share a lot in common with accommodations. But there are two key distinctions between making accommodations and UDL. First, assessment accommodations are made for individual students as a way to provide access, whereas UDL is a way of designing the assessments for *all* students. Second, assessment accommodations are selected based on previously demonstrated needs, but UDL is designed from the outset with the assumption of variability in mind. In other words, we know students in our classrooms have differing strengths, preferences, and gaps. We can be proactive by designing our assessments for this variability, rather than designing more rigid assessments for which we then need to make special accommodations and modifications.

The most common assessment accommodations found on IEPs and 504 plans are having tests read aloud and extended time (Burns et al., 2020). But what if we didn't time any of our students' on-demand work? Or what if we allowed anyone additional time when they needed it? If speed isn't critical to the essential understanding of the lesson, extended time for all does not compromise the standard—it does not modify it in any way. And if we offer this for everyone, we now don't need a special accommodation of extended time for anyone in this class.[1] We have removed a common barrier. This is UDL.

CASE STORY

In the past, Ms. Talbert assessed students' ability to support a claim with evidence by assigning a research paper. The rubric included requirements for the type of claim, a minimum number of sources of evidence, clarity, organization, grammar, the citation style, how long the paper should be, and a deadline. The instruction during class involved engaging mini lectures that brought in current events, one-on-one conferencing with students to mentor their progress, and lots of small-group work and work in pairs to develop their papers. With everyone working on the same task, though, the goal of instruction and the target in students' minds seem to be focused on the paper, rather than the true learning intention. Ms. Talbert began to jot down all the ways we can show we are adept at the skill of supporting a claim with evidence. The research paper is only *one option* for how to do so, and she wanted to make sure her students really had the ability to transfer and use their understanding in many contexts.

As Ms. Talbert reflected on the success and challenges of students' writing their research papers in the past, she recounted many students who had incredible skills at persuasive speech because they truly had a deep understanding, not only of how to support a claim with evidence, but also of how to use evidence effortlessly within

(Continued)

[1]*Note:* It remains important to document the need for extended time for students who have a label recognized by IDEA and will need this as an accommodation on state or national testing in the future.

(Continued)

informal conversation. Looking back, she could see that these students, some of whom did not perform well on the written paper, had developed skills that far surpassed what most students achieved during the course. For some of the students who performed poorly on the paper, their speaking skills were at a level much higher than their writing skills. This was particularly true for several students who had IEPs she could remember, but was also true for many more. Ms. Talbert remembered a student who was newer to English in her class a few years ago. He had a hard time with the paper, but had strong skills in what she was trying to assess. Ms. Talbert realized that the requirements of the paper kept more than a handful of students each year from showing the depth of their understanding and skills.

Ms. Talbert began mapping some of the ways that students could show their ability to support a claim with evidence. As she thought about the students in her class now and those from years past, she identified options that she believed some of her students would prefer. She wasn't sure, yet, if she planned to open up all of the options, but she wanted to generate a robust set from which to choose.

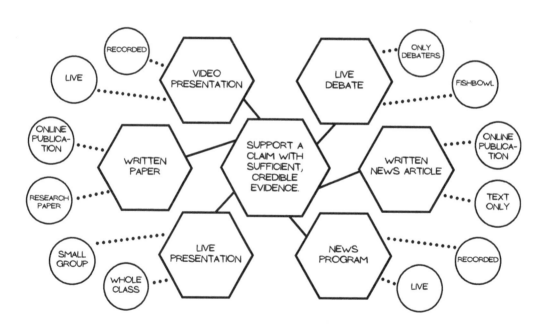

Does Choice Stifle Growth?

One of the most common questions I am asked about multiple means of action and expression is, "If we always give students the option, and students who don't prefer to write opt out of writing, how will they learn this skill?" This is an important observation! It's necessary that students have experience and support to build skills in many types of expression. By all means, ask students to write, to speak, to listen, to create, to compose, to perform, and so forth, liberally! Stretch them as appropriate, and give them feedback on all of these ways of expressing—*as a part of their learning experience.* But when it comes time to *assess,* give all the options you can. If you are assessing the ability to write clear, cohesive paragraphs, then you are free to give all the options except not to write paragraphs. If you are assessing students' ability to solve problems that involve multiplying fractions, then you have all the options available to you except those that don't involve multiplying fractions. Essentially, what is "fixed" is the skill or understanding you are measuring, but all of the other factors involved in showing that are "flexed." By removing the barrier of confounding variables, every student is able to shine! Each student, building on their areas of strength and interest, can show what they understand and know and can do, while integrating the unique parts of their personalities and experiences that make them who they are. Only by inviting and celebrating this diversity of strengths can we truly understand our students' learning and, more importantly, know them as the wonderful individuals they are on their learning journey.

 ACTION

When we give options for how students can show their learning, we give them their best chance at success. Check off the following modes of assessment you have used. Highlight the ones you have not used (or haven't used often) but would like to try. Add your own ideas to this list based on the variability you have seen in your students, this year and in years past. With this list, create a map like Ms. Talbert's for a skill you teach.

EXAMPLE MEANS OF EXPRESSING LEARNING		
☐ Video-recorded presentation ☐ Live presentation to the class ☐ Live presentation to a teacher	☐ Physical model ☐ Illustration online ☐ Illustration on paper ☐ Essay ☐ Skit or play	☐ Physical performance ☐ Sketch notes ☐ Service activity ☐ Live interview ☐ Audio interview

(Continued)

(Continued)

EXAMPLE MEANS OF EXPRESSING LEARNING

☐ Live presentation to an external audience	☐ Revision or improvement of an existing product	☐ Live demonstration
☐ Live online presentation	☐ A written story	☐ Video demonstration
☐ Written product	☐ Solved problems	☐ Drawing or diagram
☐ Text on a website	☐ Newly created problems	☐ Completed project
☐ Infographic online	☐ Multiple solutions to a problem	☐ Video interview
☐ Infographic on paper	☐ Informal group discussion	☐ Verbal response
☐ Multimedia presentation	☐ Lead a discussion	☐ Text response
☐ Individual conference with a teacher	☐ Visual art product	☐ Response with a gesture or image
☐ Written answers	☐ Hand-drawn graphic	☐ Musical performance
☐ Lesson taught live to another person	☐ Narration	☐ Spreadsheet, table, or matrix
☐ Audio recording		☐ Computer-generated graphic

CASE STORY

Ms. Talbert knew that some students showed their best work by writing about it, others by speaking, and others through producing a creative product. She provided options for students to show their learning over time, and she allowed students to add to those options. One group of students chose to present their skills on evidence by creating a video news report with examples and non-examples. As long as the students could show their learning at the expected level, she was completely open to how that looked.

For Jayson, a student in her class who has intellectual disabilities, Ms. Talbert incorporated an idea she learned last year from a special educator. She used parallel skills to use the activity to work on goals Jayson has. Jayson is incredibly social and is working on putting several sentences together on a single topic. Ms. Talbert gave Jayson the choice of topic. When he could not identify a choice, she gave him the choice between three topics. Jayson presented in front of the class several sentences on the people in his family.

Three students in her class are new to English and were not confident enough to participate by speaking in front of the class, or even in a small group. Ms. Talbert gave these three students the option to listen to the group, have the discussion recorded for translation with technology, and to give a written or verbal contribution just to her. She realized that an adaptation of these options also would be useful for the introverts in her class, and especially for Charlene, who has social anxiety.

Ms. Talbert was unsure how what she was doing with all students would look when it came time to assign a grade, but she was confident this was the right direction for classroom assessment.

SUMMARY

Multiple means for expression is, in my experience working with schools, the least often naturally used principle of UDL. But this principle is every bit as important as the other two. By not providing students with options for showing what they know, understand, and are able to do, we introduce significant barriers to many students in our class. The concept of "construct validity" is crucial for us to understand as we add options for students to express their learning. Fortunately, once we add to the options in our lessons, we can use these options year after year, building on them for ever-increasing access. In mapping an individual skill or understanding from a standard to the numerous ways a student can demonstrate the skill or understanding, we welcome and acknowledge individual preferences, personalities, cultures, experiences, and diverse strength and needs each of our students have. We want to do more than prepare students to do well on tests and follow the rules; we want to prepare them to use their voice in the world and *make* the rules.

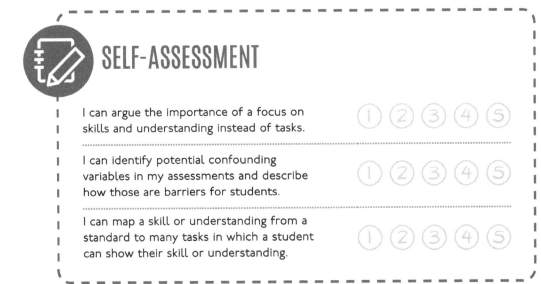

SELF-ASSESSMENT

I can argue the importance of a focus on skills and understanding instead of tasks.　① ② ③ ④ ⑤

I can identify potential confounding variables in my assessments and describe how those are barriers for students.　① ② ③ ④ ⑤

I can map a skill or understanding from a standard to many tasks in which a student can show their skill or understanding.　① ② ③ ④ ⑤

CHAPTER FOUR

Engaging Classrooms

Create Environments in Which Students Are Curious, Interested, Focus, and Persist

WHEN THE BEHAVIOR CHART DIDN'T WORK TO KEEP STEPHEN ENGAGED, MR. KRAUS DETERMINED THAT HIS CLASS WAS JUST BORING.

Learning Intentions	Success Criteria
I am learning about strategies to use to "hook" students' interest in the learning experience.	I can identify strategies I've used to hook students' engagement, and how to balance participation to hear each student's voice.
I am learning about how to use clarity, choice, and relevance to keep students engaged in learning.	I can identify strategies I've used and new strategies to try for maintaining students' interest within my lessons.
I am learning about ways to balance participation so that each student's voice is protected and heard.	I can identify specific challenges to hearing each student's voice in lessons I've taught before and select or create specific strategies to use in the future.

"10% of your grade will come from your participation." How many of us read this on a college or high school syllabus? And how was participation defined? No one needed to have it explained; it meant voluntary verbal participation in class, or "speaking up" in class. This requirement can be stressful not only to those who have social anxiety but those who are natural introverts, those who are new to the language of instruction, and those who already, because of past experiences with exclusion for any of the ways we've discussed, are uncomfortable using their voice in this public, verbal way.

We all know the student who speaks aloud in front of the group is not always the most engaged student. Extraversion is not the same as engagement, and engagement is what we really care about. There are many ways students can engage in the content and conversation of a class; participation isn't "one size fits all." Those of you reading this book span the range of intro/extroversion. Extroversion does not make one a better educator, and it doesn't make a learner a better student. Our classroom practices and ways we measure and support engagement need to be safe for all learners, whether they are comfortable or able to participate by speaking in front of the group or not. Speaking up in class is not a proxy for engagement.

But every teacher can relate, with occasional difficulty in gaining and maintaining students' engagement. "He just can't sit still." "She never has what she needs to get started with her work." "He won't finish anything without 20 reminders to get back to work." "He's off in space somewhere half of the time, not at all with the class." When a student is having trouble engaging in the classroom, do we catch ourselves attributing the problem to the student? After all, engagement is a behavior, and behaviors are a choice, right? But what if we reframe our dilemma with engagement?

Surely, you can remember a college lecture or two where you had trouble staying awake and on topic. As excited as we are as teachers about our content or lessons (and this energy does go a long way in garnering student interest), not all students share in our enthusiasm. We—and our students—all have topics we prefer more than others. What if we instead ask what the students' behavior says about our teaching? Sometimes, the difficulty isn't the student at all—it's that we weren't engaging enough! Our charge, then, is to find a way to deliver each lesson in a way that captures each student's curiosity and sense of wonder and show the relevance and importance to their everyday lives or interests.

WHY ENGAGEMENT MATTERS

Our students' focus, participation, and interest in the activities of their learning are what we call "engagement" (Posey, 2019). But the benefits of engagement extend far beyond what we can see in the moment. Beyond getting through a lesson or class-room routine, engagement serves a broader purpose, over time, of developing self-directed learners. This impact is lasting and can change the way they approach learning for a lifetime (Concentration/persistence/engagement: $d = .56$).

ENGAGEMENT

$d=.56$

-1.00   0.0   1.50

In an engaging classroom, we intentionally build student interest in culturally responsive ways and build self-regulation skills within our students to engage and persist. Our goal is that by providing these *external* means to secure and maintain their engagement, over time, students will develop their own *internal* curiosities in content that interests them and be driven to engage independently in learning, with no external supports.

The reasons for engaging students are not simply to keep a student involved in a lesson. Our long-term goal is for students to gain the skills of curiosity, focus, persistence, and self-regulation. Self-directed learners focus their attention in order to reach a goal, and they do so, not for a grade, but solely for the desire to learn. The four steps of progression toward self-directed learning (adapted from Hidi & Renninger, 2006) are

1. Initial interest, prompted by a teacher,

2. Sustained engagement, prompted by a teacher,

3. Internally driven engagement, and

4. Long-term, internally driven reengagement.

Teaching students to be self-directed is probably more important than the specifics of the last lesson any of us taught (self-directed learning: $d = .67$), and so our efforts to engage students matter.

SELF-DIRECTED LEARNING

d=.67

-1.00   0.0   1.50

REMOVING BARRIERS
TO ENGAGEMENT

There are countless reasons students may not be engaged, and those reasons are contextual. At any given point in time, a student in your class may find the work to be too far beyond their current skills, and they don't have the confidence they can do it. Another student's relationships with friends and loneliness may be weighing heavily on their mind. One may not feel a sense of belonging because they are excluded by their classmates because of their race. Another one may be bullied by others in the class because of their gender identity. Another may have experienced a traumatic event at home last night. A student could have depression or anxiety that is interrupting the ability to interact with others in the class. Another may be new to the language of instruction and is having difficulty just grasping the task. A student may not have the tools or strategies to cope and persist when the content feels too hard.

Unfortunately, we have a history of using grades as rewards and punishments in order to shape students into compliance.

But compliance isn't even the goal! We aim to develop our students to be the movers and shakers, and the risk takers—the opposite of a default of compliance. Engagement is not as simple as "some students are engaged and others aren't." Engagement is fluid, differing by student, by day, by week, by content area, class composition, and even by teacher.

REFLECTION

When you think about the students in your classroom, how do you know when they are engaged? For those students who have difficulty with engagement at one point or another in their day, what are some of the reasons "behind the scenes" that you think are contributing?

_____

_____

_____

_____

_____

To engage each student, we have to presume variability in students' interest and plan our engagement strategies with the least engaged student in mind. The student who finds history boring is on our mind as we think about how we will engage in our next history lesson. We prepare to engage students in the math lesson with the student in mind who is afraid of math and says he's "bad at math." The student who hates school is exactly who we are planning to engage as we design our next language arts lesson. If we can garner *these* students' interest and support them to feel confident in these lessons, we've probably engaged all of the students in the class.

The "Hook": Securing Interest

REFLECTION

Take a moment to reflect on a favorite lesson from your childhood; a lesson that immediately got your attention and has stuck with you all of these years. Describe this lesson.

_____

_____

_____

_____

_____

In your reflection, perhaps the content was something with which you had a strong emotional connection. Other teachers have shared stories of fascinating materials, very difficult challenges that they were finally able to conquer, teachers doing things that were silly or unusual that grabbed their attention. What no one ever mentions in these lessons is sitting and listening to a lecture, watching the teacher solve a problem on the board, or reading a piece of text and answering questions on a worksheet. Our teachers immediately hooked us by getting our attention in some way. If you ever have trouble gaining enough interest to get anywhere with your students, return to the trifecta of novelty, enthusiasm, and relevance.

REFLECTION

Think about the most engaging teacher you ever had in school. Now think about their verbal and nonverbal language that made them engaging. What are 10 words or phrases you'd use to describe this teacher?

I'll bet most of you used words like these: warm, funny, kind, gave eye contact, cared, enthusiastic, unpredictable, practical.

Enthusiasm isn't the whole picture, but it sure is important! Do you remember the 1980s movie, *Ferris Beuller's Day Off*? If you've seen it, you no doubt remember the boring economics teacher played by Ben Stein. "Anyone? Anyone? Beuller?" Find a video online if you haven't seen it. It's easy to put our finger on a boring lecture! The lesson: even if you aren't feeling totally energetic about a lesson or on a particular day, you have to "fake it 'til you make it!" Don't curb your enthusiasm! It's the animated nonverbals, bright eyes, the movement around the room, removing the barrier of a desk or podium, the intonation in our voice, and making warm eye contact with our students. It's our positive energy! This isn't to imply we all have to find our inner Lucile Ball, but that we definitely don't want to drift into the lane of the boring economics teacher, either.

Novelty is also an important part of that "hook" (Palmer et al., 2016). When our students are curious, their learning explodes (curiosity: $d = .90$). I remember a lesson in eighth grade that really "hooked" our class. This was the now popular lesson for teaching skills of expanding our written language with details by interpreting literally students' directions to do something. In this lesson, my eighth grade teacher used peanut butter sandwich making as the task. She stood in front of the class with a jar of peanut butter, knife, bags of bread, and a plate. And we all know how this goes, right? Some of the directions led her to put the jar of peanut butter on top of the bag of bread. Others caused her to put the knife in the jar and then use it to roll the jar around on a slice of bread. The class roared with laughter, was curious about what was happening, and worked collaboratively to think about language and revise the directions to achieve the desired result—a recognizable peanut butter sandwich. The lesson included novel materials, was funny, and was definitely unexpected! And our teacher was completely energetic about it. Novelty and humor are two sure-fire ways to "hook" our students. Humor alone isn't going to have an impact on student learning, but any time we can choose something a student is already interested in or something silly or novel, we are more likely to spark their curiosity and it's easier to lead them down the path of learning.

CURIOSITY

d=.90

-1.00   0.0   1.50

Balancing Novelty With Routine

Although novelty is a useful tool to capture students' interest, when everything is novel, the day can feel chaotic and overwhelming. Classroom routines and protocols are a simple way we can reduce cognitive load for students to engage. Imagine going to work each day and not being sure in which classroom you'll be in that day, what the schedule is for the day, and how the classroom space will be arranged and equipped when you arrive. You'd probably get through it, but you'd have to exert a lot of energy just thinking about how to organize yourself, your teaching, and the environment all day. What an unnecessary distraction this would be!

Established routines of the classroom or task support students by taking away the need to learn a new approach each time and can instead focus on the more cognitively complex parts of the task. The routines established in the protocols of a workshop model of writing are an example of this. Each time the teacher moves the class into a writing activity, the students already have experience with the flow of the work. Because students are not distracted by having to think about where they will go, how the prompts will look, or what the expected responses will be, they can focus on the writing task in front of them.

Provide Relevance

Most of you have probably at some point tried to persuade a young child to eat a vegetable they don't like (or think they don't like). It can be monumentally difficult to entice that first bite. So, what do we do to make the veggies more appealing? Exhausted families everywhere have learned that when we pair the vegetable with cheese, or ranch dressing, or "sneak" the veggie in a dish they do like, they are much more likely to have a taker. In some ways, engagement is like the ranch dressing. The learning intention is still there, but our goal is to drench it in so much delicious "dressing," that no one could resist. Just as this is more difficult with some foods than others, making certain lessons interesting is easier than it is for others. But when we can find ways to attach the learning experiences we plan to students' existing interests or goals they've set for themselves, we have built relevance and are well on our way to meaningful engagement.

How often have we heard a student ask, "Why do we have to know this?" or say, "We'll never need this again." Sometimes students feel like they just have to get through the lessons, units, or course. Sometimes *we* feel like they just have to get through it (insert your least favorite outcome or standard to teach). How can we find the value and relevance to help students see this? Connecting the learning experience to something that has meaning for students is important to securing their interest. By connecting to students' prior experiences or offering provocations, students see the relevance of content they may not normally see the need to learn.

Often, relevance starts with asking students to reflect on a memory. "What are some of your family holiday traditions?" We build on this relevance by posing provocations for students to reflect upon. "Think back to a time you were afraid. How did you get through that experience?" "What was something that was very hard for you to learn but now you are really good at? What strategies did you use to accomplish the goal? How might those strategies apply to something you are learning now?" Asking students to recall a memory and then applying that connection to new content not only gains engagement but serves as a mnemonic to make information more accessible. Connecting learning to students' prior knowledge makes a difference in their learning (integrate prior knowledge: $d = .93$).

INTEGRATE PRIOR KNOWLEDGE

–1.00	0.0	1.50

Teachers can also show relevance through creating an engaging, shared experience to build upon. This could be accomplished by showing a video, using field experience, or allowing exploration within the classroom. We can all recall a lesson that stuck with us because of the relevance we saw to our lives. One of my colleagues, Nicole, described a lesson from when she was in school that caused her deep reflection. This was an activity in which the class used surveying equipment with the guidance of their teachers to lay out the form of slave trading ships and then were asked to lie down in the amount of space listed in ship logs in the way that slaves would have been loaded. They lay like sardines, crammed in for only a few minutes, but it was enough to begin to imagine the horrors of the passage across the ocean. Their teachers asked them to imagine that they couldn't speak the language of their captors, the person next to them passing away on the journey, hearing a loved one crying and being unable to see or get to them. The lesson built relevance through a shared experience and provocations, and its impact has never left Nicole. Let's consider how creating a shared experience could look at multiple grade divisions.

GRADE	LEARNING INTENTION	LEARNING EXPERIENCE
High school	I am learning about the differences between modern and historical language in the arts.	After reading *Romeo and Juliet*, the teacher shows her class a film that is a modern-day adaptation of the play. Students create their own modern adaptations of another of Shakespeare's works.
Middle school	I am learning about the concepts of kinetic and potential energy.	Students explore energy with blocks, toy cars ramps, marbles, dominoes, and simple pulleys. They use a Rube Goldberg machine.
Elementary school	I am learning about the states of matter.	Combining colored water and cornstarch to make a strange new substance that is semisolid. Students create illustrations or models and explanations, either written or verbal.
Preschool	I am learning to use lots of words to describe things, to sort based on size, and to cooperate with my friends.	Using pumpkins the class chose at the pumpkin patch, as well as pictures that the students took, students move between stations, sorting pumpkins and describing them.

In all cases, a shared experience of something novel sparks student interest for a new challenge. Yes, each of these skills could have been approached with a traditional reading and classroom lecture or discussion but, now, the students are more invested. With their interest piqued, teachers are able to provide them with a challenge or series of challenges creating a shared goal for them to reach individually or in groups.

The "Grip": Maintaining Engagement

Although it takes a bit of creativity, the hook is usually the easy part of engagement. But the hook only gets us so far. It's *maintaining* students' engagement and persistence that's the real challenge. We've all felt the frustration of "pulling out all the stops" and still having students lose interest. Sometimes, it feels like there are two types of students—the engaged ones, and the disengaged ones. You know what I'm going to say about that by now: this is a false dichotomy. Not only is this a false dichotomy; this is a skill we can teach. Three powerful strategies we have as teachers to maintain student engagement and propel them forward to become self-regulated learners are

1. The clarity we have with students with outcomes and criteria,

2. The choices and autonomy we give to students, and

3. The voice we give each student.

Give Clarity in Outcomes

When instruction is *driven* by outcomes, students are more likely to stick with the learning experience, because their eye is on the prize. This level of focus on the outcomes should be present in every lesson we teach. I'm embarrassed to recall some of the lessons I delivered early in my career, almost 30 years ago. I remember so many exciting, engaging, entertaining, hands-on lessons that certainly had a hook and even kept students engaged. I even found standards to connect. But there were more than a few lessons that were just entertaining and devoid of any real assessment. I'm sure students learned from these lessons, but they would've been so much more powerful if I'd let the outcomes *drive* the lessons. Outcomes-based learning has a significant impact on student learning (outcomes-based education: $d = .97$).

OUTCOMES-BASED EDUCATION

-1.00	0.0	1.50

The outcomes we identify are the basis for the success criteria we communicate with students. At the beginning of each chapter in this book, there are learning intentions and success criteria. You are able to see exactly where you are going with the chapter you're about to read and what you should be able to do by the end. The content of the chapter is always in service of those intentions and corresponding criteria. There is no mystery in the intention of the chapter or how you should evaluate your learning. At the end of each chapter, you are asked to revisit the success criteria to determine your own understanding and needs. Success criteria give students the understanding about where they are going and what they are to achieve.

SUCCESS CRITERIA

d=.88

–1.00　　　　　　　　　　　0.0　　　　　　　　　　　　　　　　1.50

Supporting students to have a full understanding of the learning intentions and success criteria, though, requires much more than posting them in the classroom. Dialogue with students about the meaning of the learning intentions and success criteria is necessary to ensure they really understand where they are going. Students should be able to state in their own words the success criteria for what they are learning. They should know how success at each step of the way will look and feel (Hattie, 2016). Being crystal clear about the success criteria sets the stage for students to self-regulate—to be able to self-monitor their progress toward the goal and make decisions about their actions and what they need. This is likely one of the reasons that success criteria are such a strong predictor of student success (success criteria: $d = .88$).

When we're clear with learning intentions and success criteria, we can keep students with us and support their persistence. This clarity has the potential to accelerate learning (teacher clarity: $d = .84$). It may feel like we have so much to accomplish that we don't have time for dialogue on learning intentions and success criteria. But clarity has a significant impact on student learning, so the dialogue is, in fact, as an investment. Students who are clear on the destination can approach tasks with the end in mind.

TEACHER CLARITY

d=.84

–1.00　　　　　　　　　　　0.0　　　　　　　　　　　　　　　　1.50

Give Choice

One of the easiest ways to secure and maintain students' engagement is by giving students lots of choices. And the research around choice is rich: Students who have choice and feel autonomy in their learning are more likely to see the value of a lesson (Deci et al., 1996), spend more time and effort in learning tasks (Flowerday & Schraw, 2000), are more likely to complete the tasks, and may perform higher (Patall et al., 2010). Student choice is among the most fundamental features of developing engaging classrooms because of its role in building intrinsic motivation and self-directed learning. By giving choice, we build students' sense of autonomy, we bring relevance to our instruction, and we give access to differentiated learning experiences that match students' strengths and current needs. Choices can be minor such as which materials they would like to use, do they choose to work alone or in a group, the order in which they choose to complete the tasks within an activity or the activities within a class period. Or they can be more significant, such as choosing the topic of a paper or project or choosing the method of expression of what they've learned. In general, there is nearly always an option for choice within a given task.

Using the same scenarios as above, let's take a look at ways a choice can be included to further engage students within the activities for each grade level. We want to think about both trivial choices—just choices to hook interest but also choices that are more significant for building autonomy.

LEARNING INTENTION	LEARNING EXPERIENCE	OPPORTUNITIES FOR CHOICE
I am learning to use lots of words to describe things, to sort based on size, and to cooperate with my friends.	Multidisciplinary centers using items and pictures gathered from a class trip to the pumpkin patch	1. Choosing the order in which to attend centers 2. Choice of center partner 3. Opportunities for choice in how to present information learned or materials to use within activities (i.e. choice of pumpkins and gourds with which to make patterns, choosing which measurement tools from a variety to show the teacher

(Continued)

(Continued)

LEARNING INTENTION	LEARNING EXPERIENCE	OPPORTUNITIES FOR CHOICE
		which pumpkin is the biggest and how you know, choosing how to decorate your own jack-o-lantern)
I am learning about the states of matter.	Models and materials in solid, liquid, and gas forms	1. Choosing to work individually or in pairs 2. Choosing the examples of states of matter to explore and materials to use 3. Choosing how to illustrate, model, or demonstrate the phases of matter (physical model, poster, slide presentation, etc.) 4. Choosing how to explore the concept further
I am learning about the concepts of kinetic and potential energy.	Exploring energy with blocks, toy cars ramps, marbles, dominoes, and simple pulleys	1. Choosing groupmates 2. Choosing where to work in the room 3. Choosing which materials to use to explore kinetic and potential energy 4. Choosing the design of the machine 5. Choosing applications to explore further
I am learning about the differences between modern and historical language in the arts.	Creating a modern-day adaptation of one of Shakespeare's works other than Romeo and Juliet	1. Choosing the play for which you intend to create a modern-day adaptation 2. Choosing to work in groups or individually 3. Choosing which format you will create (skit, video, written adaptation, graphic novel 4. Choosing your personal target goals to address within the project

Most students don't experience an abundance of opportunities for choice each day in their classrooms (Deci & Ryan, 2002; Otis et al., 2005). And, unfortunately, choice-making is another area in education in which there are inequities. Although choice benefits all students, it seems the students who need choice the most are the ones least likely to receive the opportunity. Often students who are from low-income families, those who are below grade level, and those who have IEPs are given the fewest choices (Flowerday & Schraw, 2000). Ironically, for students who have IEPs that impact their ability to engage, providing choices is actually an evidence-based intervention that supports improvement in their engagement (Shogren et al., 2004).

Occasionally, a student's choices may have to be limited. For example, a student with an IEP may need to join a certain group because they will receive specially designed instruction in that group beside peers who also need to work on a particular skill. It's important to remember to provide other opportunities for choice whenever we are forced to limit one for a student. Likewise, it's important that, if a student has to be part of a group for an extended time for a reason such as this, that the tasks within that group should be as engaging as those in other groups, even if the content is challenging—especially if the content is challenging.

ACTION

Think of an upcoming lesson you'll be teaching in your class. Try to recall one that does not currently include a lot of student choice, and one that historically you've had difficulty engaging some students. This does not have to be a lesson that all students struggled to engage, but even if a few students needed engagement support, especially if these are students who already experience inequities, this is a good one to choose. Next, consider the challenge, or problem, or learning experience students have to explore the concept you are teaching. If there isn't already an opportunity for student-guided exploration, select one that you can add. Finally, generate options for choices you can give students within this learning experience.

(Continued)

(Continued)

LEARNING INTENTION	LEARNING EXPERIENCE	OPPORTUNITIES FOR CHOICE

As choice helps us to secure interest and students experience success, the payoff continues in maintaining engagement. Choice in the classroom is the gift that keeps on giving! In terms of maintaining engagement, though, not all choices have the same impact on autonomy and engagement. Less "weighty" choices, like where to sit or choosing the order in which to complete several tasks, may offer some benefit to engagement, but students also need more choices throughout the day that are more than simple preferences to arrive at a real sense of autonomy and intrinsic motivation. It's the resulting success students feel from more significant choices that serves to maintain interest.

The autonomy students experience in environments with a lot of choice also leads to an internal locus of control in which the student takes ownership of their learning and recognizes the control they have over their learning and outcomes (Rotter, 1954). We all know that wonderful feeling of accomplishment we have when we choose a tough challenge, persist, and conquer it. A sense of autonomy leads students to be motivated by this satisfaction they feel from having persisted and accomplished tasks related to their goals (Evans & Boucher, 2015). And, remember, it is that internal locus of control that causes us to dream big and make it happen. Supporting students to develop a strong sense of autonomy and internal locus of control will serve them the rest of their lives and is as important as anything else we teach.

CASE STORY

As Ms. Talbert prepared her next lesson on teaching her students to support a claim with evidence, she planned stations for her students to deepen their skills. She wanted them to grow in their ability to use multiple criteria to evaluate the credibility of sources they found. To maintain her students' interest, she wanted to embed as much choice into these stations as feasible. At one station, students will be using a Padlet to watch video clips from the media of adults making claims. The students will record their review of the evidence backing the person's claim. Students in a second station read sections from news articles and highlight claims that have no evidence to support them. In the third station, students work independently to continue research on their own claims.

Ms. Talbert gave students a choice board in each station to give them options of how they grouped, which resources (videos and news articles) they used, and how they would record their thoughts (annotated images, Padlet, written paragraphs, video). When she presented the options to the class, Germain asked, "Ms. Talbert, can we work with someone when we're doing our own claim research?" "Sure, Germain. Just make sure both people in the pair have equal time. Use a timer to give each person 10 minutes to talk and get feedback on theirs, and save 10 minutes at the end to work by yourself." Ms. Talbert wanted to honor the choice and also keep students focused on the outcome.

Hear Each Student's Voice

Putting into place protocols to balance participation is an action we can take to ensure all voices are heard, including those who are the loudest, most public, quickest processors and responders, as well as those who are the quietest, most private, and respond after more time or careful thought. There are many strategies we can use to balance participation in our classrooms. Balanced doesn't mean everyone speaks equally, or is expected to do so. Balancing means equity of *opportunity* to contribute. Using both small- and large-group configurations offers more opportunity for each student to have a voice. For students who are less comfortable participating by speaking in front of the whole group or asking questions in that format, protocols for balanced participation give every student the chance to be heard. Consider ways you use parameters for paired or group work like prescribing a guaranteed amount of talk time for each student, turn taking, giving options to be heard through means other than speaking, and time for silent processing.

All of the protocols below offer the opportunity to balance participation so that all voices are heard. Because of its potential to accelerate learning, I want to highlight the jigsaw protocol of cooperative learning we all know and love (jigsaw: $d = 1.20$).

JIGSAW

-1.00	0.0	1.50

The jigsaw method is impressive in its ability to increase student learning, but it also gives each student a valued voice in their home group as they summarize and lead dialogue about what they learned. Because they are in small groups, the comfort level for participating increases for many students who may not prefer speaking in front of the whole class. For students who need support because of language differences, more significant cognitive differences, or other accessibility needs, one of many supports can include pairing a student with another home group member to participate together to an expert group.

EXAMPLE PROTOCOLS TO BALANCE PARTICIPATION AND AMPLIFY VOICE	
Jigsaw	Teacher introduces a topic with several subtopics. Students are divided into "home groups," and "expert groups," and each member of the home group is assigned a subtopic. Students then group homogeneously into their "expert groups," and study their assigned subtopic through research and dialogue. Then they return to their home group to take turns teaching the group about their area of expertise.
Quick sort	Each person in the class has a group of 3–5 sticky notes. After given the prompt, students independently and silently write one idea per

EXAMPLE PROTOCOLS TO BALANCE PARTICIPATION AND AMPLIFY VOICE

	sticky note. Either in small groups or as a large group, students put similar ideas together. The first person puts their sticky notes in a central location, but spread out. Then, students each take their sticky notes and put them with an existing one that is similar or create a new category. The result is groupings of sticky notes into themes. Students can come to consensus on the names for the themes. Padlet offers an online alternative.
Think, pair, share	In pairs, students consider a question that is posed. Students think silently about their response and jot notes if they wish. Partners have a specified amount of time to respond. Partners take turns with their response.
Talking object	Students are only allowed to talk when holding the talking object. Using a talking object with small groups or in pairs ensures that each student has a turn to use their voice.
No hands up wait time	Students are prompted to wait before inviting their responses. This gives voice to those who process more slowly, are new to the language, or who prefer to pause before responding.
Chalk talk	Students respond silently, somewhere central (like on chart paper on a wall, butcher paper on a table, Flipgrid, or Padlet). Platforms like Padlet offer the additional benefit of letting students choose what type of response they'd like to include (written, video, voice).
First word, last word	The small group listens to or reads a passage silently and annotates and highlights. They number off, and the first person summarizes their learning from the passage. Each group member has the same amount of time to talk. In order, each person takes a turn adding their thoughts. The person who started concludes the meeting with their final thoughts and how they have changed during the group meeting.
Peer feedback	Partners work together to review work and offer feedback. Norms include being kind, helpful, and specific. Partner A either reads or listens to partner B's work. Partner A offers feedback. Partner A responds to the feedback. Partner B records notes. Partners swap roles and repeat.
Paired annotating	Pairs individually read a section of text and annotate the main idea in the margins for each paragraph. They circle any words they don't

(Continued)

(Continued)

EXAMPLE PROTOCOLS TO BALANCE PARTICIPATION AND AMPLIFY VOICE	
	know. After both are finished reading and annotating, they compare their circled words and main idea. They find the meaning of words they did not know and come to consensus on a main idea.
Quick mix	Students are given a question or idea to consider. Everyone thinks individually and silently about their responses. Students are given a partner and have 20 seconds each to share the response. They then transition to a new partner and repeat.

Cooperative learning protocols are strategies we should be using in every classroom, both for their effects on learning and for their utility in giving each voice value (cooperative learning: $d = .45$). For each of these protocols to protect each student's voice, it's essential to think about the group composition and anticipate any barriers to inclusion and voice. For example, assigning all students a number and making choices about how students find a partner can prevent the discomfort many students feel in reaching out to another person in the class. Being attentive to the norms of collaboration and circulating the room to support students in their collaboration skills is a role you play as facilitator. In every decision we make about engaging groups and hearing each one's voice, it's essential that we're cognizant of the emotional safety of our environment.

COOPERATIVE LEARNING

d = .45

-1.00   0.0   1.50

CASE STORY

Throughout the year, as Ms. Talbert's students continued to develop in the ability to support claims with evidence, students explored and analyzed the implications of baseless claims made online through fast-spreading social media. Because claims made in the media often spark a lot of emotion, conversation can get out of hand in large groups. She also knew that many members in her class would be able to participate easier by being in a small group.

Ms. Talbert used an activity to break students into small groups, and she intentionally used strategies to invite and balance participation within the groups. The strategy Ms. Talbert used was "First Turn/Last Turn" with a talking stick. Not only did Ms. Talbert want to teach the skill of supporting a claim with evidence, but she also wanted to support her students in developing conversational turn-taking, self-management, comprehension, interpretation, application, relating, integrating, metacognition, and appreciation of others. She gave her students these directions after breaking them into groups of four, and each person was assigned the letter A, B, C, or D:

"Silently and simultaneously, each of you will read one section of text from the news article on yesterday's events in Birmingham. Each section is marked with the letters A, B, C, or D. You'll read the section corresponding to your letter. As you do so, you'll each highlight three or four items that have particular meaning for you. You have the option to listen to the section on your computer with your headphones or silently read the section to yourself." Ms. Talbert also used an online translation app to have the article ready in Spanish for Maciel, a student in her class who was newer to English.

For Jayson, his friend DeShawn read a sentence of the text to him. Jayson used a highlighter to highlight a word. DeShawn read the word, "yesterday," that Jayson had highlighted and asked him to use "yesterday" in a sentence. Jayson started the sentence for him, "Yesterday, Ms. Talbert..." and Jayson finished the sentence. "...she taught us about working together." DeShawn told Jayson he would help him remember his sentence when it was time to share.

After a few minutes, Ms. Talbert asked each team member to share one of their items while holding the talking stick, but not to comment on it. Moving from A to D, each person passed the talking stick and simply named the item that meant something to them. In turn, each group member shared one of their items. Next, she asked groups to repeat the process, but this time share for I minute, their thinking on the topic. Other group members could ask questions for clarification, but not for commenting. Then the talking stick was passed to the next person.

Later in the year, the class moved into discussions and debates using other strategies to balance participation and created online news programs in which they presented claims with evidence. At times, Ms. Talbert encouraged the students to choose a position opposite from their own and build an argument with evidence. She wanted them to see social issues from others' perspectives. Again, she used small groups and pairing to create a safer space for students who may have felt threatened or uncomfortable in large-group conversation.

The class discussions did become close to tense at times when students had conflicting opinions on politics, all supported by evidence they deemed credible. But with Ms. Talbert's formative feedback and guidance, the groups used the class norms of collaboration to work through the dialogue in a productive manner. Ms. Talbert had posted the norms of collaboration prominently at the front of the classroom and referred to them frequently before group work, particularly for

(Continued)

(Continued)

controversial topics. She beamed with pride as she watched the groups use the norms of collaboration to navigate difficult topics, strong opinions, and conflicting evidence with skills many adults are lacking.

By the end of the year, Ms. Talbert rarely needed to provide any guidance for groups to use the norms. They spoke confidently, supporting their opinions and claims. She had established a culture of safety in her classroom, evidenced by every student having and using their voice. By teaching empathy through the way she organized her lessons to see others' points of view, students provided safety for one another to voice their own thoughts.

 ACTION

When we focus on engagement of the least engaged student, we make sure we reach every student. Check off the following engagement strategies you have used. Highlight the ones you have not used (or haven't used often) but would like to try. Add your own ideas to this list based on the variability you have seen in your students, this year and in years past.

1. **Use novelty and enthusiasm to hook students' interest.**

   ☐ Use humor.

   ☐ Do something unexpected.

   ☐ Start with a thought provoking or controversial statement and dialogue.

   ☐ Use a short video that captures interest.

   ☐ Include opportunities to engage with by investigating, reflecting, doing, making, creating, dialoguing.

   ☐ Have students move about the room during learning.

   ☐ Be animated in your voice, facial expressions, and body language.

2. **Connect the purpose of the lesson to something of current relevance and value to students.**

   ☐ Tell a story that is relatable to your students.

   ☐ Relate the lesson to a current event.

    ☐ Connect the lesson to pop culture for students' age group.

    ☐ Dialogue about the purpose of the lesson (beyond posting or reading the purpose).

3. **Demonstrate clarity of intentions and criteria for success.**

    ☐ Describe purpose for upcoming learning using text and voice.

    ☐ Lead an activity to help students understand the purpose of learning.

    ☐ Clarify vocabulary by highlighting words and leading groups to discuss the meaning.

    ☐ List, describe, and provide examples of success criteria for the learning.

4. **Provide many choices to students about their learning, from simple choices to significant ones.**

    ☐ Students select the topic for their reading, research, or writing.

    ☐ Students choose roles within small groups.

    ☐ Students choose learning activities or assignments from a menu.

    ☐ Students add to a list, perhaps started by a teacher, on the ways they can show their learning.

    ☐ Students codesign a lesson.

5. **Protocols for equitable voice.**

    ☐ "No hands up" wait time.

    ☐ Jigsaw

    ☐ Chalk talk

    ☐ Journal

    ☐ Individual conferencing

    ☐ Quick sort

    ☐ Think, pair, share

    ☐ Talking object

    ☐ Round robin

    ☐ First word, last word

    ☐ Peer feedback

    ☐ Paired annotating

    ☐ Quick mix

SUMMARY

Not all students are equally engaged for a variety of reasons. Those students who are already marginalized for one reason or another are often the students who need more support to engage. Sometimes, a lack of engagement happens because the invitations to participate are weighted toward extroverts and student who have a lot of social capital. Our strategies for engagement should be designed to engage whoever is the least actively engaged and can be used and iterated each year. We begin by supporting students to be engaged in learning situations by providing a safe environment, novelty, relevance, and enthusiasm. We then keep students engaged and persisting in the learning environment by being clear about learning intentions and success criteria, giving ample choice, and each student a voice. Classrooms designed for the universal engagement of all students encourage students to take ownership of their learning. When the "vital content" is clear as well as the expectations for success, students are free to make choices that suit their preferences to meet those expectations. Students are encouraged to make plans, set goals, and collect data so that they always know where they stand. Our ultimate goal is that by providing these external means to secure and maintain their engagement, over time, students will develop their own interests and have enough curiosity and interest to guide their own learning for a lifetime.

SELF-ASSESSMENT

I can identify strategies I've used to hook students' engagement, and how to balance participation to hear each student's voice.

I can identify strategies I've used and new strategies to try for maintaining students' interest within my lessons.

① ② ③ ④ ⑤

I can identify specific challenges to hearing each student's voice in lessons I've taught before and select or create specific strategies to use in the future.

① ② ③ ④ ⑤

CHAPTER FIVE

Developing Expert Learners

Facilitate Content That All Students Can Access, Remember, and Understand

WHAT'S NECESSARY FOR SOME
IS GOOD FOR ALL.

Learning Intentions	Success Criteria
I am learning about how to use modes of representation to make instruction accessible.	I can identify and use multiple modes of teaching to bring accessibility needed for a diverse group of learners.
I am learning about strategies to use to support my students' memory and retrieval of information.	I can design lessons and units that include specific strategies for representing content in a variety of ways.
I am learning about strategies that support my students' conceptual understanding.	I can design lessons and units that include specific strategies for aiding a diverse group of students in understanding the concepts I teach.
I am learning about making content accessible to students who have more significant language or learning differences.	I can design lessons that include layered success criteria or parallel success criteria for students who have more significant learning differences.

NO LEARNER IS AVERAGE

A common faulty categorization of student variability in the past was that some students were gifted, some had learning difficulties, and most were somewhere in the middle. This over simplification of student variability was reflected in rigid instructional practices designed to reach most of the students most of the time. Historically, instruction was aimed at "teaching to the middle," to the "average" student. Ability grouping was used to meet the needs of students with learning differences. As we know, this model of replacing core instruction for all with a leveled approach resulted in an ever-increasing gap for students who had learning needs. For students who were new to the language of instruction, language support was offered in a separate setting, which is neither most effective nor promotes a sense of belonging that is so important. Although language needs and learning needs are certainly very different, this exclusion is a commonality they shared. With students in both of these groups, there was a need to demonstrate a level of achievement to justify the right to be included into core instruction.

This approach to grouping and exclusion is neither equitable nor inclusive. And this is not how variability in skills within students works! Your learner inventories have illustrated and the research supports that each class is a set of individuals each with their own set of strengths, needs, interests, and approaches to learning. Not one of them is average and, in fact, there is *no* average student. This is true with every single class of students. As Todd Rose so eloquently describes in *The End of Average* (2016), the idea of there being an average person is really a myth. Instruction that is aimed at the average student is designed for no one, and works well for *no student.*

MULTIPLE MODES FOR ACCESSIBILITY

Universally designed classrooms represent content using multiple modes of teaching to make sure students across the range of variability can access and make meaning from learning experiences (modality: $d=.55$). When it is the expectation rather than exception that all students will be learning differently and this is a natural part of the planning process, flexibility becomes the norm. Besides, it's much more difficult to individualize support after the fact than it is to represent content in multiple ways from the beginning. Remember the historic building in Chapter 1?

MODALITY

$d=.55$

-1.00   0.0   1.50

Using combinations of spoken words, images, mental images, video, text, objects, students' primary language, and movement to represent content leads to instruction that's more accessible to *all* learners *all* of the time. The potential result for students with IEPs is a reduced intensity and frequency of individualized instructional supports, because many of those measures are already woven into the fabric of the classroom. (We'll address individualized supports and intervention more in the next chapter.) For example, we can make audiotext available to complement a written text. This simple act supports students with visual impairment, those needing decoding or comprehension support, English language learners, and those who simply take in information more efficiently through listening. Most students who benefit from accessibility and support measures don't have IEPs. Using multiple modes of instruction means no one is overlooked, IEP or no IEP.

Not only does combining modes of instruction provide access to the content, but using multiple modes also reduces the cognitive load for students, increasing their understanding of the content. Some students may be able to read grade level content, but it takes a lot of cognitive energy to do so for long periods of time. This can be true of many students, including those who are reading in English but are newer to the language. Pairing text with other modes like verbal teaching, images, graphics, animations, and video, lighten this load for students so comprehension is maintained.

Throughout this book, I've used metaphors, images, mental images, icons, and graphs to represent content visually and with text. There is a checkmark icon that accompanies the banner for learning intentions and success criteria. There are illustrations at the beginning of each chapter that offer a glimpse into what the chapter is about. There are illustrations for concepts. Effect sizes are represented in the same way and with a graph. There are banners and icons for case stories, reflection, and action in each chapter. Each chapter concludes with the same visual for a self-assessment. And colors for icons and banners are consistent throughout the book. These visuals combined with the text help you mentally organize the reading, and in cases like the effect size graphs and various illustrations, the visuals help you comprehend concepts. Mental images like the one of the historic building and an upcoming one about a ramp, the stories, like Ms. Talbert's, with examples, all serve the purpose of understanding the content and concepts we teach. Investing effort in multiple modes of instruction during our lesson planning minimizes the need for special accommodations later, because instruction was designed to be accommodating of a diverse group of strengths, needs, and backgrounds in every group of students.

REFLECTION

Think about a class you had in college where most of the way the professor provided instruction was through reading text. There was little verbal teaching or use of video or other modes. Perhaps this worked well for you, but it

(Continued)

(Continued)

definitely didn't work for everyone. Maybe it didn't work well for you at all! What could this professor have added to the reading to help students understand and apply the information better?

_____

_____

_____

_____

_____

Verbal Accessibility

Verbal teaching is at the core of every teacher's practice. We are able to quickly adjust and support students by checking for understanding and then adding new examples, engaging in dialogue, and supporting individual students "on the fly." But, teaching content, a concept, or skill by *only* giving information verbally doesn't work for everyone. For learners who need more time to process information, or those who need more support for memory and other less "visible" needs, adding modes to verbal information can be just as necessary. Adding text, graphics, icons, images, video, symbols, and tangible objects are all options to increase accessibility of verbal language.

The skill of listening isn't simple. It's a complex skill that students have to be taught. Advance organizers are a perfect example of support to verbal language that is a research-based intervention for some, but is useful for everyone (advance organizers: $d = .42$). And creating and giving an advance organizer that all students use is no more difficult that one given to a single student to use. Prewritten notes with blanks for main concepts or words give students a scaffolded way to listen without the need to have strong verbal processing or advanced note-taking skills to be successful.

ADVANCE ORGANIZERS

–1.00	0.0	1.50

A simple way to help students customize how they take in spoken information is using options to activate closed captions and transcripts with video to represent what we are seeing and hearing. YouTube videos, most televisions, and videoconferencing plug-ins all have this capability. Closed captioning historically was considered as support only for Deaf people and those with hearing impairment. But many of us benefit from or even prefer closed captions. At the moment I'm writing this, I'm flying in a plane and have forgotten my headphones. If I were to watch a movie, captions would be my way to access the movie. And if you've ever wanted to watch television or a video while there is a sleeping baby in the room or next room, you may have used these features to keep the volume muted or low. For students who are new to a language, subtitles are often available in the student's primary or preferred language to accompany video. And using subtitles and captions in the new language also supports language development. Those who have better processing speed with printed text, when using new vocabulary, and even in a room where quiet is needed are also contexts in which closed captioning are beneficial to learning.

Other Sound Accessibility

Much of the information we take in on a daily basis is through sound beyond spoken words, like notifications pinging on our phones, babies crying, doors shutting, clomping, water pouring, fires crackling, and car engines roaring. Sound is not easily accessible to Deaf people and people who have hearing impairment, so adding other modes, like sign language, text, haptics, and images are necessary. With our mobile phones, we have the option not only to change text displays, but there are options to add tactile output, like haptics and vibrations, in order to receive alerts or feel our hitting of visual keys. We have the option to raise and lower volume. These tactile outputs ensure greater accessibility for Deaf people and those who have hearing impairment, but we all use these features for discreet use of our phones.

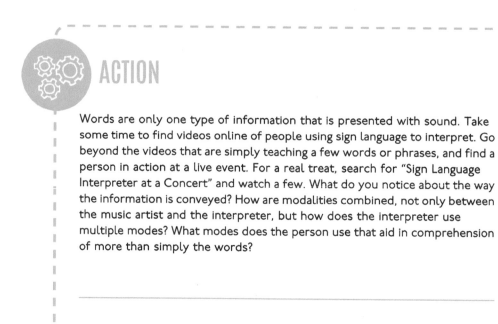

ACTION

Words are only one type of information that is presented with sound. Take some time to find videos online of people using sign language to interpret. Go beyond the videos that are simply teaching a few words or phrases, and find a person in action at a live event. For a real treat, search for "Sign Language Interpreter at a Concert" and watch a few. What do you notice about the way the information is conveyed? How are modalities combined, not only between the music artist and the interpreter, but how does the interpreter use multiple modes? What modes does the person use that aid in comprehension of more than simply the words?

_____

_____

_____

_____

_____

Text Accessibility

Text is a specific type of visual information that requires students use multiple, complex skills at the same time. With print materials, such as a book, the text and way the content is available is fixed. There is only one way for students to access the material with only a book available. Just as adding text to verbal instruction aids in understanding, adding spoken language to text supports understanding. It's the same combination of modes and this pairing has reciprocal effects on each mode. Many technologies allow for flexibility in access to and learning from text. There is tech, for example, to change the Lexile or language of written text. There are programs that read aloud to students and cue students to read along by highlighting each word read. There are options for choices of text size, ensuring contrast between the background and text, avoiding red/green combinations to accommodate for color blindness, using a highlighting color for emphasis, and using fonts that are easily readable. Hyperlinks or the "lookup function" on most computers can take students to definitions and example usage of vocabulary. Smartphones have accessibility features built in to customize, like changing the brightness, text size, ability to zoom in, or to speak the text on the display. And, of course, there is the prolific use of emoticons to clarify meaning that is often misinterpreted without them.

I used to use a lot of cursive in my presentation slides because I was fond of the visual appeal of cursive, but the use of cursive has waned in the past decade. Many people didn't have cursive instruction in school and find it more difficult to process. If someone is devoting a lot of cognitive space to reading cursive, there is less space to processing the content. Such a simple change in font type makes the information more accessible for everyone.

Offering students the choice to listen to information, with or without the text displayed, supports understanding for students who are new to the language, process spoken information quicker than text, and is an option for those whose reading skills need support. Allowing time for and giving the option for repeated reading also builds both decoding skills and comprehension. We don't want to hold a student's ability to think and learn about complex content because they are newer to the language or for other reasons have difficulty reading and understanding text.

For example, we can give the option to work in pairs or groups so one student gets to read aloud and others are able to listen and read along. These strategies are useful for wide variation, including those with more significant cognitive needs.

Computers and phones offer screen reading options and text-to-speech features, although digitally produced verbal is not rich in expressing with intonation in the way a person is able to use. The teacher's simply reading the information to everyone is basic but engaging and effective. Sometimes, the simplest solution is the best solution.

Other Visual Accessibility

Visuals such as pictures, graphics, video, and visual art are wonderful additions to text and verbal teaching to aid in comprehension. But visuals can be just as inaccessible to other students. Students with visual disabilities or those unfamiliar with the type of graphic presented benefit from combinations of modalities to understand or comprehend visual information. Visual art can be complex with subtleties and many interpretations that are difficult to understand, depending on ability, cultural background, or experience. Adding modes to bring accessibility to the visuals, again, can be useful for any student. Descriptions of images, including alt text in online images, provide visual accessibility. Highlighting patterns and relationships in visuals by adding annotations in text or verbal form or organizing the visuals in multiple ways scaffolds the use of visual information.

Language Accessibility

For the most part, schools in the United States have English as the only or primary language of instruction. Even though there are many languages represented in most schools, the curricular materials don't often reflect this diversity. For students new to the language of instruction, the ability to comprehend instruction is compromised without access to their primary language (or languages), visuals, and other support. There is often an assumption that if we make curricular materials available in the student's primary language, this will impede their ability to learn the new language. This assumption is incorrect. To the greatest extent possible, we do need to provide the support of parallels in the content in students' primary language, including if the student uses sign language. Remember, American Sign Language does not translate to sign language beyond American English, and different forms of sign language are needed for Deaf students who are new to English.

For students who have gained fluency in social communication of the new language, having parallels for academic vocabulary may be necessary for comprehension. These parallels can include combinations of modes—primary language text, new language text, verbal primary language, visual maps and diagrams, graphics, photos, and so on. Figurative and slang speech, idioms, colloquialisms, and jargon of a language, group, or region is often inaccessible to students new to the language, but also other students as well. Specific parings of modalities that support language accessibility and acquisition follow and meet the accessibility needs of many students, not only those who are new to the language of instruction.

REFLECTION

Recall a concept you have taught your students recently for which you mostly taught verbally. For example, you may have asked students to read a short passage and then engaged them in dialogue about what they read in order to teach the concept. What are additional modes you could add to that lesson to increase students' comprehension of the verbal teaching? How do you think that would have impacted learners in your class who need support to access information via spoken words?

_____

_____

_____

_____

_____

LEARNING TO LEARN

Gone are the days when we thought students were successful if they memorized content and played the game of school well enough to earn high grades. We know that to be successful beyond the walls of a classroom, students have to gain the ability to apply knowledge, understanding, and skills and need the mental strategies to process information. They have to be able to prioritize, summarize, categorize, contextualize, compare, contrast, and the like. Most students don't have a well-developed range of these strategies, the processing speed to use them on demand, and a keen sense of when to apply them. Well-designed instruction not only teaches content and surface knowledge, but also guides students to go deep with their learning of their own cognitive processes.

Metacognitive Strategies

Metacognition is thinking about our own thinking and making decisions about how we approach content based on how we each learn best. Metacognitive strategies are the methods we use to help students monitor their own learning, determine what they understand and don't understand, and use the strategies that work best for themselves to improve. This includes the tools we give students to help them understand their own thought processes. When students know the conditions under which they learn best, and strategies to use when learning is difficult or frustrating, they are on their way to being self-directed learners. Students with strong metacognitive skills are the ones who become expert learners (metacognitive strategies: $d = .60$).

METACOGNITIVE STRATEGIES		
	$d=.60$	
–1.00	0.0	1.50

We all have different strategies to approach our learning as adults. Where do you like to be when you are learning something new? In a quiet space, or in a busy space? Music or no music? Do you learn well and easily from a book? Or does it work better for you to have or create examples? Do you need to process out loud with others? And what do you do when you feel overwhelmed? What keeps you going? Our answers to these questions vary, so there isn't one set of strategies that will work with all of our students. Our task, then, is to guide students to engage in thinking about how they learn best.

As students develop their metacognitive skills, they asking questions of themselves during their learning, such as "What am I doing now to learn this?" and "Is this helping me to understand and remember this?" If the answer is "yes," the student takes note of what is working and how it can be used in other circumstances to improve learning. If the answer is "no," what they are doing now is not sufficiently helping them to learn, the follow-up question becomes, "What else could I be doing instead?" Metacognition prevents students from inefficiencies in studying, like by reading the material over and over and getting nowhere, and instead figuring out what approaches to learning work best for them (Perkins & Salomon, 1989).

We give students multiple options for how to take notes, how to study, how to approach a problem, and we guide them in reflection on these strategies to identify what works best for them. When a student is feeling overwhelmed, challenge them to reach back to a memory when they felt the same way and got through it. Ask them how they might apply that strategy now.

We have to explicitly teach and scaffold metacognitive skills. We start by pausing and giving students questions and time to reflect on their learning at three stages: (1) Before their learning to plan, (2) During their learning to monitor themselves, and (3) After learning to evaluate the outcomes. The objective is to build metacognitive routines that become a part of how students approach all learning—eventually without any teacher support. The support is unlikely to be there in college, so we need to start teaching this early.

EXAMPLE QUESTIONS AT EACH STAGE OF LEARNING		
Before Learning	**During Learning**	**After Learning**
I can plan for my own learning.	*I can monitor my own understanding during learning.*	*I can evaluate how I learned, what worked, and what didn't work.*
What are the learning intentions of this lesson/task? How do they connect to my personal goals?	What questions are arising for me during the class session? Am I writing them down somewhere?	What was today's class about?
What do I already know about this topic?	How interested am I in this? How confident am I in my learning? What could I do to increase my interest and confidence?	How did the ideas of today's class session relate to previous class sessions?
How could I best prepare for the class?	Am I struggling with my motivation? If so, do I remember how this class connects to my goals?	To what extent did I use resources available to me?
Where should I sit and what should I be doing (or not doing) to best support my learning during class?	In what ways is the teaching supportive of my learning? How could I maximize this?	To what extent did I successfully accomplish the success criteria of the lesson?
What questions do I already have about this topic that I want to find out more about?	In what ways is the teaching not supportive of my learning? How could I compensate for this?	What do I need to actively go and do now to get my questions answered and my confusions clarified?
What are all the things I need to do to successfully accomplish this task?	What strategies am I using that are working well or not working well to help me learn?	What did I find most interesting about class today?
What resources do I need to learn this? How will I make sure I have them?	To what extent am I taking advantage of all the learning supports available to me?	What worked well for me that I should use next time?
How much time do I need to complete the task?	Which of my confusions have I clarified? How was I able to get them clarified?	What did I hear today that is in conflict with my prior understanding?

EXAMPLE QUESTIONS AT EACH STAGE OF LEARNING		
Before Learning	**During Learning**	**After Learning**
If I have done something like this before, how could I do a better job this time?	Which confusions remain and how am I going to get them clarified?	What did not work so well that I should not do next time or that I should change?
How much time do I plan on studying? Over what period of time and for how long each time I sit down do I need to study?	What other resources could I be using to complete this task? What action should I take to get these?	What mistakes did I make? Why? What confusions do I have that I still need to clarify?
Which aspects of the course material should I spend more or less time on, based on my current understanding?	Can I distinguish important information from details? If not, how will I figure this out?	What will I still remember 5 years from now that I learned in this class?
Why is it important to learn the material in this course?	What is most challenging for me about this task? Most confusing?	If I were to teach this lesson, how would I change it?
How am I going to actively monitor my learning in this course?	What could I do differently during the learning to address these challenges and confusions?	What advice would I give a friend about how to learn the most in this class?

Source: Tanner (2012).

Visual Organization Tools

Do you have students who can't seem to remember their materials or to do tasks or get "stuck" while engaging in a learning experience? Do you know students whose lack of organization and planning are getting in the way of their learning? Of course you do! For students who need support following through with multiple steps of a task, this is usually more about executive functioning than it is about trying to get out of the task. Our abilities of executive function dictate how we take in information and determine how we will execute a response. And just like all other types of variability, our students vary in their executive functioning as well.

ADVANCE ORGANIZERS

d=.42

-1.00   0.0   1.50

Among the simplest strategies students can use to assist their own learning and memory are visual organization tools such as the use of sticky notes, phone reminders, and using concrete items to help visualize abstract concepts. Using online calendars and reminders can push the cognitive load of remembering to do a task out of the way so more is available for the actual engagement and learning. Teachers frequently give instructions for the multiple steps of a task, verbally. Not all students process this information at the same speed and same accuracy. Checklists and visual schedules are both examples of tools to accompany explicit prompts for each step to help students visually organize time, tasks, and locations. Providing students with options for what they will use, and time to use these, pushes their metacognition to discover what tools are best for them. Advance organizers that we all use are examples of external organization tools. Advance organizers, like graphic organizers to help lay out papers before writing them, are research-backed organization tools that improve students' learning (advance organizers: $d = .42$).

REFLECTION

When you think about how you manage your learning, tasks, and approaches to learning, what works best for you? Which organization tools and memory strategies do you wish you'd been taught at a young age to accelerate your own learning?

_____

_____

_____

_____

STRATEGIES TO ENHANCE MEMORY AND RETRIEVAL

Mnemonics

One set of metacognitive tools with an incredibly strong research base in supporting memory is mnemonics (mnemonics: $d = .80$). Mnemonics pair something that is difficult to remember with something that is easy to remember. Some of these include tactile tools where motions or our bodies help us remember things, like using the peaks and dips of the knuckles to remember which months have 31 days and which are shorter. There are letter strategy mnemonics such as "Please Excuse My Dear Aunt Sally" to remember the order of operations when completing math problems where the first letter of each word in a silly phrase represents a step in the sequence; in this case parentheses, exponents, multiplication and division, addition and subtraction. We probably all learned musical notes, the color wheel, and planet names with this type of mnemonic. But there are many other types of mnemonics in which we combine something easy to remember with something new or difficult to remember.

MNEMONICS

$d = .80$

-1.00   0.0   1.50

For example, with the keyword strategies we create an image to help remember the meaning of the keywords in a concept. For instance, if one were trying to learn the vocabulary word jettison which means to cast out excess, they might create a visual of a Jet with people pitching cargo out of it to help them remember its meaning. I'm sure I'm not the only one who has trouble remembering "to-do" items without a list. Lists help many of us sleep at night, knowing we won't forget these tasks. But sometimes these needed tasks occur when we are driving or in the shower and can't grab the phone or paper and pen to add them. I use a keyword visual mnemonic strategy to help me remember items I need to add to the list. Today, I remembered that I needed to buy Magic Erasers at the store and that I needed to call San Diego State University for help with my library login. Between then and the time I was back at my desk, I knew I'd forget. I visualized a magic (for the erasers) log (for login) in my head. The log was wearing a magic hat and had a magic wand. I didn't forget to add the two items to my list. Any time we can pair something new to memorize or remember with a mental image, sound, or other "shorthand," we improve retrieval. Ultimately, we want students to be able to create their own mnemonic strategies for retrieval.

Metaphors and analogies are a special type of mnemonic and serve a role in aiding understanding and memory. Like the letter mnemonics we all remember, metaphors and analogies help us attach new concepts to concepts we already understand. Memory metaphors have long been used in cognitive psychology to explain complicated concepts (Roediger, 1980). The use of metaphor is even included in the Common Core standards for writing.

So far in this book. I've used old buildings and ramps as analogies for understanding the differences between UDL and differentiation, and these evoked mental images. Metaphors and analogies can both aid in our understanding by breaking down concepts, but they also serve as a tool for memory retrieval. When students learn to create their own analogies and metaphors to understand more deeply and remember their understanding, they move closer to becoming independent expert learners.

Peer-Assisted Learning

One of the challenges teachers often describe is how exactly to support both students who have mastered an understanding or skill while also meeting the needs of students who need more time or support to catch up. Peer tutoring is a research-based answer to this challenge (peer tutoring: $d = .51$). Peer-Assisted Learning Strategies (PALS) is a specific peer tutoring practice in which the teachers pair students who are proficient with a subject with students who need support as study partners, and partners take turns in their role as tutor and tutee (McMaster et al., 2006). As an educator, you already know the value of teaching on your own learning. And the research is clear on the impact of PALS: this practice accelerates the learning of both the tutor and the tutee. Students learn from their "tutor," and in the role of "tutor" the teaching reinforces their own learning, making this is both a logistical solution as well as a learning solution.

PEER TUTORING

d=.51

-1.00   0.0   1.50

Supplying Prerequisite Knowledge

For students who lack the background knowledge that's necessary to access new information, they begin the learning at a disadvantage with barriers already in place. Barriers can also exist for students who have the background knowledge but don't identify it as relevant. Content is more accessible and comprehensible by students when we first give them the prerequisite knowledge.

The semantic elements of words, symbols, numbers, and icons that we use are not always accessible to all students. To ensure accessibility for students with varying backgrounds, languages, and lexical knowledge, we link key vocabulary, labels, icons, and symbols to alternate representations of their meaning, like with a glossary, a graphic, a diagram, or chart. In universally designed lessons, teachers pre-teach vocabulary, concepts, and symbols in ways that connect to students' experiences and what they already know—including what they have learned in other subject areas. They break down complex terms, expressions, or equations into smaller pieces of words, symbols, and expressions. In making these connections in content we also need to intentionally show students how the mental processes connect—how their understanding and skills they learn in one context "greases the wheels" for other understandings or skills and helps them transfer those to other subjects and areas of their lives.

Summarize and Outline

When we think about students who easily master new content, they have the ability to distinguish main ideas and the most critical information from what is supporting information, and even unimportant or irrelevant. Because students who have this skill quickly recognize the most important features in information, they are able to use their time efficiently. They are at an advantage in all content areas because of this skill (outlining and summarizing: $d = .72$).

OUTLINING AND SUMMARIZING

-1.00	0.0	1.50

For this book, there is an accompanying glossary and outline for note-taking. Within the book, there are boxes to prompt reflection and self-assessment. We can scaffold the skill of summarizing and outlining by highlighting new vocabulary and associated meaning. Offering guided notes in which words or phrases are missing help students engage as they follow and remove the need for advanced note-taking skills in order to access content. This option does not mean that students aren't taught and learn the skill of summarizing and outlining. We must teach that skill explicitly. But until they gain expertise with note-taking we remove the barrier to learning other skills or gaining understandings. Said another way, if a student doesn't yet have proficiency with identifying the most important information, we still want them to be able to access and make meaning with the content. Teachers can accomplish this by highlighting the features (visually and verbally) that matter most while deemphasizing those that matter least.

Scaffolding

We all know about and use scaffolding continually in our classrooms. In this strategy, a teacher moves from offering a lot of support and then gradually fades that support to build students' independence through success at each building small step along the way. Sometimes we do this by only giving small amounts of information at a time and then more as students have learned each part. "Chunking" information is a type of scaffolding we have all used. We group information in a long chain of items to make them more manageable, like we do with telephone and social security numbers. And we each have seen the results of this practice that are affirmed by the research (scaffolding: $d = .58$).

SCAFFOLDING

$d = .58$		
-1.00	0.0	1.50

Parents and caregivers naturally scaffold teaching their children. When you were first learning to tie your shoes, your parents probably tied your shoes for you—to be able to get out of the door and on with the day. They'd describe the steps, and you started trying. They gave you as much help as you needed and gradually reduced their help as you learned.

You probably have students in your class who give up easily. They don't have a strong internal locus of control or self-efficacy. You have other students who have more significant cognitive support needs. Although we all use scaffolding, we can intentionally infuse this strategy as universal design for learning (UDL) into more of our teaching of content and skills where even a few students noticeably need the support. Content areas in which students routinely become frustrated or give up are both opportunities to scaffold as well as to teach coping skills for when the work feels too difficult.

 ACTION

Think about the students in your class, and reflect on a student you know who has significant learning differences. Recall a lesson you've taught that has an active learning component—a shared learning activity. In the past, what have been your thoughts on including students with significant learning differences in this lesson? How might you use layered and parallel criteria to adjust the

(Continued)

(Continued)

success criteria, connecting appropriately challenging goals for the student, and promote their meaningful participation in this activity? Use the table below to record your ideas.

LEARNING EXPERIENCE	LAYERED SKILLS

LEARNING EXPERIENCE	PARALLEL SKILLS

Understanding Nonverbal Communication

In watching the videos of the sign language interpreters, you no doubt noticed the use of exaggerated facial expressions and body language to add to the meaning that was expressed in the words. Much of the meaning we make in interaction with other people is through facial expressions and body language—nonverbal communication. These are critical components of being an effective sign language interpreter.

Interpreting social cues, facial expressions, and body language, though, requires not only accommodations for people who have low or no vision, but also for those who need support in making meaning of these types of expression. People who are on the autism spectrum, those with nonverbal learning or social communication needs commonly require support for interpreting social cues. Many students need scaffolding to learn the meaning of facial expressions and body language, regardless of a label or identified need.

Different cultures also have varying ways of communicating nonverbally, and understanding a person's visual cues can be difficult without experience with a different way of communicating. Of course, it's necessary that when we describe characteristics of a group that we avoid cultural stereotyping and, worse, make assumptions about an individual from a particular group. But it is also important that we are aware of cultural norms and differences in order to understand one another and see all forms of communication as valid.

Even what we attend to in a person's facial expressions can vary by culture. In a study conducted at University of Glasgow (2012), the researchers found that Chinese participants relied on the eyes more to represent facial expressions, while Western Caucasians depended on the eyebrows and mouth for interpreting meaning. The conclusions of the study were that cultural distinctions could lead to missed cues or misinterpreted signals about emotions. And cultural differences are not only seen from country to country, they are present between regions of countries, cultural groups within countries, and even between families.

The concept of context also has been used to describe a general way of communicating and using nonverbals across cultures. A *high-context* culture is one that depends on a great deal of nonverbals, subtleties, and cues that are not expressed with words. In a *low-context* culture nonverbal communication is less important, and explicit use of language is where most meaning is communicated (Rüttger, 2018). Although cultures usually have characteristics of both high and low context, there are differences. This requires that the person receiving information from a person who is more high context is able to infer the information that is implied by the nonverbals. For example, if a student were to hop out of their desk and dance around to communicate engagement, a teacher may interpret this as disengaged or off task, when in fact the opposite was true. Another example of a missed cue could be a student who needs help, instead of asking with words, uses facial expressions and looking toward the teacher to ask for help. We also see this in students who are quieter or have social anxiety. Regardless of the reason, a teacher who is from a low-context culture may overlook either student. Many white Americans are part of a low-context culture that could misinterpret high-context students' communication. Latino and African American cultures, for example, tend to be more high context. Given that the makeup of the pool of teachers in the United States leans strongly toward white females, these mismatches are likely frequent. Whether from a high-context or low-context culture or family, having self-awareness of our communication style and biases toward other communication styles is a step toward being able to communicate with all students in ways they understand.

PLANNING FOR MORE SIGNIFICANT LEARNING OR LANGUAGE NEEDS

When content is delivered intentionally to facilitate understanding, teachers segment or chunk the information to be delivered stopping to check for understanding, allow students to catch up, and take time to make connections. There are no secrets in equitable and inclusive settings about what is important and how things fit together. Teachers not only write the learning intentions on the board or name them at the beginning of a lesson; they engage their students in conversation about them, and they explicitly make connections using multiple modes. "How does this information relate to what we've previously learned?" "What strategies can we use to remember this new term?" All of these challenges allow students time to process and practice information while allowing teachers to hear what they are thinking before moving on to the next piece of information.

Differentiation is what we add to universal design to meet the known needs of individual students in our classrooms. Differentiating the complexity within our success criteria matters in designing classroom instruction that ensures every student learns and understands (differentiation: $d=.46$). In contrast, without differentiating complexity of success criteria, the challenges of the learning experiences are too great for some students, creating anxiety, and not enough for others, leaving them bored. In both cases, students' motivation and engagement are lessened. Boredom and anxiety both have negative impacts on learning (boredom: $d = -.33$; anxiety: $d = -.36$).

DIFFERENTIATION

-1.00   0.0   1.50

Layered and Parallel Success Criteria

Most teachers feel comfortable including students in lessons when there is not a significant gap between where the student is and the success criteria for the lesson—or even when the student has surpassed the success criteria. But many teachers do not feel confident in including students who have significant performance or cognitive differences. When we gage the level of challenge in our lessons and tailor the success criteria based on the variability in our students, we make sure the challenge we provide is the right fit to keep each one persisting (appropriately challenging goals: $d = .59$).

APPOPRIATELY CHALLENGING GOALS

-1.00   0.0   1.50

In making decisions about inclusion for students who have more significant differences, the misguided question is often, "Can this student meet grade-level expectations?" or "Can this student meet a modified version of grade-level expectations?" The answers to these questions of whether students have "earned" the right to be in the general education classroom all too often segregates students with more significant learning differences. In those times when students with more significant learning differences have a wider gap between the learning intentions and their skills, the right question to ask is, "Can the student gain valuable learning within this setting or within this lesson?" If the answer is "yes," and it almost always is, a layered or parallel approach to success criteria can bridge the gap.

Layered Success Criteria

In the image of a cake, there are three layers. All three layers are cake, and they are all part of the same cake.

LAYERED SUCCESS CRITERIA

When the success criteria are not appropriately challenging for a student, we can use a layered approach to our lessons in which we think in terms of what all students will do, what most students will do, and what a few students will do. In this way, teachers have the same learning intentions for all students (all are cake), but the success criteria are at different complexities (the different layers) (Giangreco et al., 2020). The activity and learning intentions are the same, but there are layers to the complexity. The fundamental skill or understanding of the lesson is what all students will do. Most students will be working toward the grade-level success criteria, and a few students are ready to accelerate to a higher success criteria. Before assuming the appropriate success criteria, though, it's important to ensure that a simple change in options for expression, as introduced in Chapter 3, couldn't easily be all that is needed.

CASE STORY

Ms. Talbert and Ms. Garcia met during their common planning time to think about the upcoming unit and stations Ms. Garcia had planned to think about the ways to make the content accessible for Maciel and how to aid in his understanding of the content. The two teachers had worked together for many years, and Ms. Talbert had a lot of experience with students who were newer to English. She'd learned a wealth of strategies from Ms. Garcia over the years. Ms. Talbert offered her suggestions for the upcoming unit, with Ms. Garcia as a thought partner. They quickly identified where layered criteria options were—most of which had already been built into Ms. Talbert's lessons from the past years.

LEARNING EXPERIENCE	LAYERED SKILLS
Students watch a video of an adult making a claim, discuss their thoughts and rate the adult's use of credible evidence.	Maciel watches the video ahead of time with a peer and has discussion with the peer, making notes. Maciel participates in the group activity with his notes.
Students read sections from news articles and highlight claims that have no evidence to support them.	Maciel reads a small section from one news article that has claims highlighted. Maciel underlines claims that have no evidence.
Students work independently to continue research on their own claims.	Maciel works with DeShawn to continue research. DeShawn has exceptional research skills and will be an excellent mentor as Maciel gains these skills.

Parallel Success Criteria

In this image of parallel criteria, there are three cakes on the plate. They are all cake, but they are distinctly individual cakes with different flavors.

PARALLEL SUCCESS CRITERIA

Using a parallel criteria strategy, students are all involved in the same shared learning experience (the plate). Everyone is included and an authentic member of the group (all on the plate). During the shared experience, the student with more significant needs is actively participating toward success criteria for a goal that is important for that student (their individual cake). During a lesson on gravity, for example, students may be having a shared experience (the plate) with objects in a science classroom. Most students are selecting items, making predictions, testing their predictions by dropping items, and recording the results and comparisons (one of the cakes). A student who has more significant learning differences and is not able to achieve a modification of the corresponding success criteria may be learning to label objects, to make choices using eye movements, to us a radial digital grasp to pick up and release small objects, or draw objects with a pencil (a separate cake). The opportunities for parallel success criteria are endless and open up countless inclusive opportunities for the full range of needs in our student populations. It is important, though, that we do not use parallel criteria as a default. Parallel criteria are only appropriate if layered criteria are inaccessible.

CASE STORY

Ms. Talbert and Mx. Brackenstein met after school to think about the best ways to make the upcoming unit a meaningful one for Jayson. As they thought about the upcoming learning experiences and the stations Ms. Talbert had planned, they easily identified parallel skills Jayson could target during the lesson. Ms. Talbert had not been confident in her ability to include Jayson, but as Mx. Brackenstein walked her through creating a matrix for parallel skills, her confidence grew.

LEARNING EXPERIENCE	PARALLEL SKILLS
Students watch a video of an adult making a claim, discuss their thoughts and rate the adult's use of credible evidence.	Jayson sits independently in a chair and names his friends with his communication device.
Students read sections from news articles and highlight claims that have no evidence to support them.	Jayson uses a "pencil grip" with the highlighter to highlight in lines on the news articles.
Students work independently to continue research on their own claims.	Jayson makes choices about where to sit and makes choices between independent activities with his communication device.

SUMMARY

Representing content in multiple ways brings accessibility and efficiency to our students' learning. It also brings efficiency to our planning and teaching. UDL challenges us to plan, from the outset while we are designing lessons, to intentionally give many entry points and options to all students to help them comprehend, learn, make meaning, and apply what we are teaching. The goal is to teach content, concepts, and skills in enough ways that learning is accessible to all students, and very few special accommodations or modifications are needed. Our instructional strategies plan for students who are strong readers, novice readers, confident speakers, English learners, students who know how they learn best, and those who are starting to learn about what strategies to use. We want our students to engage in "thinking about their thinking" and know how they learn best in order to make choices that work for them. We want students to set goals for their learning, know how they are doing, and know what strategies they should use. Our goal is for our instruction to be so accessible and effective that all students understand the concepts, are able to apply their learning, and have the tools to differentiate for themselves throughout their lives.

SELF-ASSESSMENT

I can identify and use multiple modes of teaching to bring accessibility needed for a diverse group of learners.

I can design lessons and units that include specific strategies for representing content in a variety of ways.

I can design lessons and units that include specific strategies for aiding a diverse group of students in understanding the concepts I teach.

I can design lessons that include layered success criteria or parallel success criteria for students who have more significant learning differences.

CHAPTER SIX

Flexible Support and Intervention

Design Support for Skills That Is Delivered in Inclusive Settings

SO CLOSE AND YET SO FAR AWAY.

Learning Intentions	Success Criteria
I am learning about the impacts of Multi-Tiered System of Support (MTSS) on how students are grouped and served.	I can describe three "nonnegotiables" of MTSS and compare and contrast those to the practices of my school.
I am learning about the roles of paraprofessionals and how to define these roles best.	I can articulate the harmful effects of one-to-one paraprofessional roles and design alternatives that work.
I am learning about what an intervention is and how it looks.	I can compare and contrast the definition of intervention to how support is provided in my school.
I am learning about coordinated small-group learning as a way to allow students to flow in and out of intervention without removing them from core instruction.	I can apply coordinated small-group learning by designing a schedule for delivering flexible, responsive intervention across classrooms.

So far, we've spent our time in this book on whole classroom efforts, preparing for the diversity in our students. This universal approach is the right place to begin to create welcoming, effective, inclusive environments that responds to a lot of needs a lot of the time. But these universally designed practices do not *eliminate* the need for additional adaptations and intervention. The group of students who needs intervention comprises not only those who have Individualized Education Programs (IEPs). Remember the false dichotomies? Many students have difficulty learning to read and do not have dyslexia. Many students feel the trauma of racisim, ableism, and other "isms" and don't have an IEP. And there are students who have difficulty with self-regulation but also don't have an IEP. Just because a student fits within a group does not mean they need intervention.

The amount of intervention a student needs is also not dictated by whether there is an IEP. A common misunderstanding is that special education equals a need for tier three intervention. But there are plenty of students newer to the language of instruction that need minimal support. And there are some who need a great deal of support. The same is true for students who have a learning difference, are on the autism spectrum, have a need for support in mathematics, and the like. Some students with labels need less intervention than some students who have the same need but no label. As we thought about in the first chapter of this book, the decisions about intervention are all about what the student needs right now—never about to which group they are a member. We'll explore this in depth in this chapter. When students need support beyond what is happening in the classroom, with excellent universal design for learning (UDL) in place, the questions become: "How should this support look?", "Do we provide support within the student's classroom or in a smaller setting outside the classroom?", and "Who provides this support?"

INCLUSION

-1.00	0.0	1.50

d=.25

So, why am I including a graph of an influence in education that has a low impact and seems to support that statement? Some may gloss over inclusion as a practice that doesn't lead to a high effect size of more than .40 and use this to back the statement that "inclusion doesn't work." Beyond that, I've heard many teachers over the years express that inclusion holds back students who don't have learning differences, and I've heard parents echo this. Although inclusion doesn't have a large effect size for the full student population, it is likely to have an effect, and most important is the direction of the effect: It is a positive effect, not a negative one (inclusion: *d*=.25). Negative impacts of inclusion on students without disabilities are a myth. And when we dig deeper beyond the broad effects on all students, we see that for most populations of students who have learning differences, the benefits are overwhelmingly positive. For example, high school students with the label of learning disability are 1.6 times more likely to go onto post-secondary education for *every core subject* area that they spend in the general education classroom (Joshi & Bouck, 2017).

Simply having students in the same physical space together isn't *really* inclusion, though. Inclusion is more than "pushing in support or intervention" into a classroom. While having all students together in a classroom fits the legal requirements for inclusion for students who have IEPs, this isn't *really* inclusion. We can still exclude students, no matter where in the building they are. And we can include students in any part of our building, too. It would be interesting to know the effect size for the influence of *real* inclusion, beyond physical placement.

I remember visiting student teachers a number of years ago, and what I saw in an elementary science classroom has stuck with me ever since. In this class, students were being introduced to the concept of static electricity and its relationship to negative and positive charge. Students experienced static electricity by rubbing an inflated balloon on each other's heads. They laughed at the resulting "hairstyles" as they experimented.

In the back of the room was a student with Down syndrome, seated with a special educator, working on different content. His teacher had a hard time holding his interest, because he was so interested in what the rest of the class was doing with these brightly colored balloons as they all interacted with one another and laughed. It's worth our efforts to put into place every instructional practice we can to ensure that all students are successful in inclusive environments. Students have a human right to be included with their peers, not excluded in the same space.

MULTI-TIERED SYSTEM OF SUPPORT

In the opening chapter of this book, you read about a Multi-Tiered System of Support (MTSS), often known as RTI[2] when discussing only academics, and MTSS when the framework is applied to a broader scope of learning, including social or emotional skills. Up until this point, we have focused on UDL—what we can do for all students to reduce barriers to their learning and expression. The strategies we have provided thus far are *tier one* strategies because they are ones we use with our entire class on a regular basis. And we design these preemptively, because we presume variability of all kinds in our classes of students.

RESPONSE TO INTERVENTION

d=1.09

-1.00   0.0   1.50

For some students, though, we do need to provide support or intervention beyond what is given to all students. Within an MTSS framework, this means we deliver targeted or intensive intervention, but we do so, to the greatest extent possible, in inclusive settings. Three key "nonnegotiable" features of MTSS are (1) the decision-making framework is applied to EVERY student, not only those who have IEPs; (2) students cannot be pulled from core instruction to receive intervention; and (3) they should be able to start or stop intervention at any point, receiving as much as they need for as long as they need. This does not mean that students can't receive small-group or individual intervention. But it does mean that we cannot pull students from any new instruction that the class is receiving to give the student intervention.

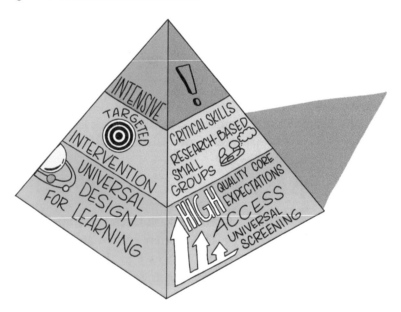

Some schools have misinterpreted "core instruction" to mean "core subject areas." In that way, schools were free to pull students from "specials," like physical education, music, and art. They pulled students from math to receive a math intervention, removed students from language arts to deliver English language support, or took them out of art to deliver a reading intervention. But this is an incorrect usage of the term "core instruction." In an MTSS model, students are not removed from *any* instruction that is core to *any* subject. So, when does intervention happen? It can happen any time this core instruction is not happening, such as during independent work. Independent work time can be formally planned for a class, group of classes, or for the school, such as in what is often called a "flex block." In classrooms where there is a co-teaching model, intervention can be fluidly infused into independent work time throughout the day.

INTERVENTION DEFINED

What Is Not an Intervention

Interventions have the ability to significantly accelerate learning. Before we define "intervention," we need to first describe what intervention is *not*. First, helping a student with homework or an assignment is not an intervention. This is a common scenario: a student is having difficulty with an in-class assignment, like responding to a series of written questions. It may be that the student needs help understanding the assignment, reading the questions, needs more time, or is having trouble getting started with getting thoughts down in writing. The student may be helped by a special education teacher in a resource room or with a paraprofessional in the classroom. This type of support is usually only available to students who have an IEP. When we think about how we often provide support on assignments to students who *don't* have IEPs, it's usually the classroom teacher who helps. The lesson here is that helping the student get through this assignment is not the same as an intervention. And who is the best person to help a student with an assignment? The person who assigned it.

Second, it is also *not* intervention to assign a paraprofessional to work with a student or group of students. Just as with the assignment help from a special educator, assigning a para-professional to a student is generally only given to those who have IEPs. Not only is one-to-one paraprofessional support not an intervention, this "so close, yet so far away" approach is actually harmful, and the list of ways in which it is harmful is neither short nor insignificant.

HARMFUL EFFECTS OF ONE-TO-ONE PARAPROFESSIONALS
Exclusion: Students who have a paraprofessional are often seated at a table separate from the rest of the class.
Dependence: Paraprofessionals often do work for or with the student, instead of teaching the skills, and the student is less likely to participate without the paraprofessional's guidance, cues, or directions.

(Continued)

(Continued)

HARMFUL EFFECTS OF ONE-TO-ONE PARAPROFESSIONALS

Harmed Relationships: Students with paraprofessionals do most things together, without other classmates, making it more difficult to have friends.

Less Teacher Engagement: Teachers are less likely to engage with a student who has a paraprofessional.

Embarrassment: Having a one-to-one paraprofessional makes students feel stigmatized and different.

Lower Quality Instruction: Many paraprofessionals are not trained or supported in their jobs.

Reduced Autonomy: Students with paraprofessionals are less likely to have and make choices.

Bullying: Students who have a paraprofessional are more likely to be bullied.

Loss of Gender Identity: Many times, students who have paraprofessionals are taken to the wrong bathroom in a building with gendered-bathrooms, because the default is to the paraprofessional.

Source: Adapted from Giangreco et al. (2005).

Having paraprofessionals in our schools is a valuable resource! When appropriate training, support, and collaboration happen, the benefits can be truly pivotal to students. The harm with the role comes when schools assign a single person to a student or a few students, and their primary job is to support that student. We know we've done it well, when we can walk into a classroom, see more than one adult, and have no idea which students have an IEP. The paraprofessional can be specially trained, for example, in intervening with a challenging behavior, or delivering reading instruction, or in meeting a student's personal care needs. But those types of support should only be given when needed, and the rest of the time, the paraprofessional is working as a classroom assistant with all students. Further, if the paraprofessional is trained to support a student's challenging behavior, that training can be applied with any student. The student who has a behavioral goal on an IEP or behavior plan is definitely not the only student who will need support for a behavior in that class-room! It's frequently true that the paraprofessional will spend more time supporting behavior of others in the class than is being spent for a student who has an IEP.

REFLECTION

Think about your experiences with students who have had one-to-one paraprofessionals. Have you noticed any of the harmful effects listed? If so, how has this looked?

_____

_____

_____

_____

_____

What Is an Intervention?

With the nondefinition out of the way, we can identify what intervention is: Intervention is systematically supporting the student to mastery on a critical skill or understanding, using a research-based practice (intervention: $d=.78$). Let's break down that definition:

Systematically
The support is being provided with intention and purpose. A team has determined the desired outcome and identified a specific program, strategy, or set of strategies that they will

implement. They implement the strategies with fidelity—checking in with one another to reflect and make sure the strategies are being used and are effective.

To Mastery

Skills progress in a path toward mastering the skill. This path begins with *acquisition*, continues to *fluency*, shifts to *maintenance*, and then expands to *generalization* (Haring et al., 1976). It goes without saying that this path is the same for all skills and for all students. There is no unique path to mastery for students who have IEPs. Remember, there is nothing about students who have IEPs that's only true of students who have IEPs. It's all about needs.

THE PATH TO MASTERY

1. Acquisition

Acquisition is demonstrated the very first time we use a skill: the very first time you took a step, said a word, multiplied two fractions, or wrote a paragraph. Have you ever learned how to do something long enough to get through a test and then completely forgot? We all have! In this case, your teacher measured only your acquisition of the skill.

2. Fluency

Once students can perform the skill over and over consistently, they show *fluency* with the skill. The first time you wrote a paragraph was probably not when you mastered this. You probably did it within a set assignment and likely needed feedback on subsequent attempts. You showed fluency when you were able to consistently write with all the requirements of a paragraph. The same is true of all skills. Language fluency and reading fluency are only two types of fluency.

3. Maintenance

When students show that they can keep using the skill beyond the instructional period, and with independence, they have reached *maintenance*. I remember learning calculus in college, and I did well in my classes. I acquired the procedural knowledge of calculus, was able to get fluent with those skills, but I did not maintain them. I definitely don't have the skills now and probably didn't two weeks after the class was over. I didn't reach maintenance. In order for a skill to be worth supporting, it has to be applicable in many situations. And the most important skills to far outlive a student's academic career.

4. Transfer

Finally, when students can take the skills they've learned and use them across a variety of settings, they demonstrate *transfer*. In reality, it matters little whether a student demonstrates a skill or understanding in a separate setting with a specialist. What matters is whether the student can use the skill in new ways or new contexts in situations when it is authentically needed.

Source: Haring et al. (1976).

Critical Skill or Understanding

Interventions are not about dragging students through assignments, tests, or homework. They are focused on skills and understandings that are transferrable across subject areas and across time. Memorizing the first two rows of the periodic table of elements is not a critical understanding. Knowing how to retrieve memory is. And knowing how to see patterns and make meaning is. Doing this with the periodic table of elements is not the only way and probably not the best context in which to teach these skills. Remember the "life changing" prompt from Chapter 3? It comes into play here, too. What will change this student's life? This is how we identify critical skills and understandings. No one wants to exert all the effort to solidify a skill with a student if it's going to have little impact on their life. And getting through a class or passing a test is not justification for a skill to be life changing. It's life changing if the actual skill is needed or likely to be needed for a lifetime, and they develop and deepen across time.

Research-Based Practice

Using a research-based practice, one that has evidence from the research that it works, is a required element to call a practice an intervention. Without evidence that a type of support works, we could be wasting the valuable resource of the interventionist, and worse, the student's time and effort. Keeping up with practice by engaging in professional journals, conferences, and work like Visible Learning and visiting the What Works Clearinghouse are the places to go for research-based practices. Remember the old metaphor, "All that glitters is not gold." The same is true for large, colorful booths at conferences and ads in professional magazines. Not every advertised program out there has strong evidence. Be a critical consumer.

INTERVENTIONS

d=.78

–1.00	0.0	1.50

Who Gets Intervention or Support?

Anyone who needs it! As we introduced earlier, not all students have had equal access to intervention and support. Historically, only students who had IEPs were guaranteed intervention. While it is true this population is the only one that is legally protected to receive intervention, we all know that to be an inclusive school that values equity, we must go beyond the letter of the law and meet the *spirit* of the law. Every student deserves evidence-based intervention and support as soon as they need it, for as long as they need it. Grouping students by which label they have, then, doesn't make sense. We should be grouping students instead to support them on individual skills as needed—and these groups are not all-day groupings in segregated classrooms for only that need.

For example, in a third grade classroom, we should not be pulling the students who have IEPs to work on reading skills. Rather, we can use small-group instruction time to provide support to *any and all* students who need support with reading. The same goes for a common high school approach to support: we should not be grouping all of the students who have an IEP and sending them to the special education resource room for help. This puts the special education teacher in the position of playing a proverbial game of "whack-a-mole," trying to meet a diverse set of needs for that group of students. This often turns into a time where the teacher is supporting homework, assignments, and test taking, none of which can be considered an intervention. There is more variation within a group of students who have IEPs than there is between this group and those who don't have IEPs. Instead of clustering students who have IEPs, we need to provide skills-based intervention when students are in need of this—and for only as long as they need this.

CASE STORY

After the final bell rang and all students had left the building, Mx. Brackenstein sat at their desk and let out a loud sigh. They weren't feeling effective at their job at all. Mx. Brackenstein had spent the better part of the day in the resource room trying to work with fifteen students who had IEPs, but all needed different kinds of work. When they weren't doing that work, Mx. Brackenstein was "pushing in" to classrooms to support individual students. Neither seemed to be working.

While Mx. Brackenstein was in Mr. Barton's room, they were able to work one-on-one with Jayson on vocabulary, but there were other students in the room who needed some type of vocabulary work who didn't have IEPs. They felt defeated that they couldn't possibly get to all of the students on the caseload every day for the amount of time the students needed. Mx. Brackenstein wasn't even sure they were meeting the requirements of what was on the IEPs. They felt better about Jayson's inclusion in Ms. Talbert's room, because they were working together to design lessons, and Ms. Talbert saw Jayson as "her student," too, not belonging to special education and Mx. Brakenstein. But most teachers didn't see it this way. They weren't sure the school even saw it this way.

In the resource room, Mx. Brackenstein felt like all they had time to do was answer questions about assignments and try to get to all 15 students to be able to help with what they were working on in other classes. There was absolutely no time in the day to use the programs for math and reading that they were trained to use. There was no time scheduled for this, either. For the students who are in the resource room, some of them don't need to be there anymore, but there is no way within the schedule to move them back to their classrooms.

As Mx. Brackenstein was leaving for the day, they walked out with Ms. Garcia, an ELL teacher. Mx. Brackenstein shared their feelings of defeat with Ms. Garcia about not being able to serve students in the way they needed. They weren't the only one to feel this way; Ms. Garcia was having some of the same problems. She expressed concern with students who need ELL support for a part of the year. Ms. Garcia felt the students who were ready to be in the class with their peers missed out by being stuck in the ELL classroom because of the schedule. Students weren't getting what they needed, and worse, they felt isolated and as if they didn't belong.

Ms. Garcia and Mx. Brackenstien agreed: no student should feel like they have to "earn their way" into a class. But neither was sure of the solution.

ACTION

Talk to an ELL teacher, special educator, or reading specialist at your school. How does a "day in the life" look and feel for them? What are their thoughts on having the time and support to do their job well? How is this related to the number of students they are assigned to support or to the way the schedule affects how they teach?

(Continued)

(Continued)

_____

_____

_____

_____

_____

WHERE DO STUDENTS RECEIVE INTERVENTION OR SUPPORT?

The experience of Norman Kunc, a well-known disability rights activist and presenter, underlines how opportunities to achieve mastery of skills and understanding in inclusive settings is often missed. Norman has cerebral palsy and reflects on his experiences as a student as he impresses upon audiences the need for all people to have an authentic sense of belonging (belonging: $d=.40$). In an interview, Norman talked about "the stairs to nowhere"—a set of stairs that his in-school physical therapist required him to climb and descend, over and over (Giangreco et al., 1993).

BELONGING

$d=.40$

| -1.00 | 0.0 | 1.50 |

Norman was pulled out of his general education classroom and curriculum for this work. Were there no natural opportunities for Norman to practice his stair-climbing skills during the day? What about getting on and off the bus? What about walking into and around the school? The skill of walking up and down stairs was a critical one, but the focus was on one specific task instead of the skill. There was no systematic approach to move

Norman to transfer a skill. When we take students to a separate room to work on a skill or understanding without being clear about the skill and making connections to how the skill should be used and supported throughout all relevant settings, we have led them up the stairs to nowhere.

REFLECTION

Reflect on how students who have need for additional support or intervention receive this support at your school. How are students grouped? Where are they served?

_____

_____

_____

_____

_____

THE SPACES IN THE BUILDING

Norman's experience parallels many types of skills and corresponding supports or interventions. I remember visiting a kindergarten class some years ago, and then going into the "OT room," where occupational therapy was delivered. Young children were in the room with scissors and sheets of paper with lines. The occupational therapist was supporting and instructing the children to cut on the lines. But cutting and other fine motor activities are a natural part of any kindergarten classroom. It's not necessary to pull students to another setting to work on this. There is nothing sacred about the "OT room." Any space in the building, including small groups in the classroom, can be used to deliver fine motor support or intervention.

We can deliver almost any type of support for almost every student in an inclusive setting. ***In fact, there should be no spaces in our buildings where only students who have IEPs or are new to the language of instruction or have a diagnosis are served.*** Did your eyes widen at that statement? If so, let's think about what that says and doesn't say. Does this mean that we never work with students in small groups? Of course not. Does this mean we don't provide intervention? No. What this does mean is that no spaces require a label to get in. Those "special education resource rooms" are simply spaces where students go to receive support. If any student can get support, and the room isn't simply filled with students with IEPs and students with dissimilar intervention needs, then it *is* a general education setting. What makes a setting inclusive is the group composition and the interrelationships of students in that space, not where in the building it is.

Do students in the classroom who don't need intervention ever benefit from working in a small group? Is it true that at times small groups might convene in a space outside of the large group in a classroom? Yes! For example, students who are working on a collaborative project and need a particular set of materials might go to a maker space to do that work. Students who are working together in literary analysis may need to have conversation out loud and need a space separate from where the rest of the class is silently working individually. And a group of ninth grade students who need reading intervention may need a separate space because it would be too stigmatizing to receive that in a small group during independent work time in a language arts class. There are many reasons students may need a smaller space to work. But none of those reasons is because a student has a label or IEP. So, should we be calling any of our spaces "special education" spaces, or "ELL spaces?" Our spaces should be flexible and not attached to labels.

We shouldn't be so naïve to believe that by changing the names of spaces that this will result in different beliefs about students who need intervention or support. In the international schools where I often work, the common language is "learning support," and "learning support teacher." You may be thinking that this is nice language, and it is. But it's only nice language to you because it doesn't imply "special education." But guess what? Over time, in places where "learning support" is the language used, if it only applies to students who have an IEP (even if the IEP is called an individualized learning plan), then "learning support" takes on the same meaning as "special education." Accompanying a change in language, which is a great idea, must be a change in the culture and the procedures. More on that in the next chapter.

One of the comments I often hear is that this all sounds great, but how does it apply to students who have multiple, significant needs who are served most of the day in segregated special education rooms. The fact is, there is still a continuum of services, from all day in a general education setting to all services being delivered at home or in a hospital. This can apply to students with and without IEPs. In those times of day when students with more significant needs may be served in a small-group setting, there are many opportunities for students without significant needs to benefit. When you thought about what is the portrait of a graduate or what we value most in our students, you no doubt thought about skills of autonomy, citizenship, leadership, empathy, and the like. What better context for all students to gain these and many other skills than when in the company of students who have more significant needs?

Just before the pandemic, our team was in a district in California conducting a review of inclusive practices. We saw such beautiful examples in some schools of all students gaining by being in inclusive settings. Yes, there was a continuum of support, but no student in the building was in a setting that only students with IEPs were served. Students with significant needs benefited from the friendship and support of their classmates. We saw students without significant support needs reading to students who did have significant needs, inviting students with significant needs to play on the playground and join groups in the classroom. Even students with the most significant needs benefited from interaction with peers in the school, and students without significant needs helped in classrooms in a variety of ways, from reading to groups of students to pushing wheelchairs. The benefits to students with significant needs was outweighed only by the benefit to the mentor and supporting students. It all felt completely natural, and for that reason, was truly beautiful.

REFLECTION

What are the shining examples you see around you in your school, around town, and in your community social circles of people with significant needs being included? Where do you see opportunities for greater inclusion?

_____

_____

_____

_____

_____

How Do We Decide When to Provide Additional Support?

We've established that labels are not the way that we determine whether students need additional support. So how do we decide. The first rule to remember is that we don't wait until a student is significantly behind to intervene (FPG, 2007). The old way of providing supports to students with the label of specific learning disability was to "wait and see." Teachers noticed that students were behind grade level in reading, for example, but it was common practice to not deliver intervention and wait until the student was in third grade to determine if there was a label and then, if that was the case, provide intervention (Wanzek & Vaughn, 2007). The contrast in outcomes for students who require reading support or language support who receive intervention beginning early versus in third grade is stark (O'Connor et al., 2014; Torgesen, 2004). When at-risk readers receive intensive intervention early as beginning readers, 56%–92% go on to achieve average reading ability (Torgesen, 2004). *Any student* at risk for reading failure, with or without a label, should receive evidence-based intervention, of sufficient intensity, and as early as possible. This goes for risk of failure in any critical skill area.

To make these decisions, we have many tools available to us. Schools have implemented screeners and general outcome measures to determine relative risk. But these aren't the only ways we can make decisions about intervention. The estimates of student achievement made by teachers help them to set expectations, gage progress, identify those who have early signs of difficulties, and inform intervention choices. These judgments come from everyday interactions with their students and observing their performance. Teachers' estimates of achievement when used to inform instruction and intervention are one of the greatest influences on acceleration of student learning.

TEACHER ESTIMATES OF ACHIEVEMENT

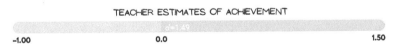

| -1.00 | 0.0 | 1.50 |

THE SCHEDULE QUANDARY

It seems simple enough: the research suggests that

1. Any student who needs intervention should get it,

2. They need real intervention,

3. Students should not be pulled from core instruction to receive intervention,

4. Small-group instruction works, and

5. Students should start and stop intervention as they need it.

Because of the compelling evidence, most educators see the value in these intervention practices, but the school schedule is often the deal killer in the logistics of making it happen when the "rubber meets the road." And it isn't only the students' schedules that are the problem; teacher schedules create difficulty as well. If we cannot pull students from core instruction to receive intervention, then when do we deliver this? The low-hanging fruit seems to be the "specials," like art, music, and physical education. But in the context of MTSS, "core instruction" does not mean "core subjects," but instead refers to the instruction that all students receive in *every* subject or time of day. What this means is that we cannot take students away from any core instruction that is being delivered to the whole class. But the gap between this research and what's happening in schools is closed when we consider new models of serving students to deliver intervention.

Many schools manage their limited intervention resources by pulling students with similar needs from core instruction into a group so the specialists can maximize their time during the day delivering intervention. This leads teachers to pulling students based on the adults' schedules instead of the schedule of core instruction delivery. In upper school, when students begin to change classes throughout the day, schools report having difficulty managing this without putting a time in a student's schedule. This means they are "stuck" in this intervention, or, more commonly, room, time all year. If they don't need an intervention at the beginning of the year, it's difficult to access that when the need arise, as Mx. Brackenstein and Ms. Garcia found. The research is clear that this "replacement model" does not work.

The summary of the schedule quandary is this: If we need to work with students who have similar needs without pulling them from core instruction, then it seems the only way to do this is classroom-by-classroom, working with the students within that room who have the same need. But sometimes that is only one or two students in a classroom. If we do it this way, there is no way the specialists can get to everyone in the school who needs support. If we group students from across classrooms who need the same type of support, then it seems impossible not to pull from core instruction. In upper school, this doesn't seem possible without scheduling a block in the day for intervention or support.

COORDINATED SMALL-GROUP LEARNING

Ample time for small-group learning has a place in every classroom and school (small group learning: $d=.47$). There is no coincidence that lecture, on the other hand, has a negative impact on learning (lecture: $d=-.18$).

SMALL GROUP LEARNING

d=.47

| -1.00 | 0.0 | 1.50 |

Using the power of small group instruction, instead of pulling students from across classrooms regardless of the instruction that is taking place, we can carve out time each day when core instruction pauses for a group of classes, or a grade level, and convene small groups that allow each student to focus on an individual priority. We should be using small-group instruction anyway, and this is about coordinating that time across classroom and using that time as an opportunity to deliver intervention and support. Students who need support with a skill can have that support, whether there is an IEP in place or not. And every student has something to work on. Some students may need to be together with a small group to work on a project, others may need time to catch up on work, still others may need the same intervention. We can meet the intervention needs in small groups when there is a need for the same intervention, and we can do so by bringing together students who need this from across classrooms without the risk of interrupting a student's learning from core instruction.

Just before the pandemic, I was working with International School of Kuala Lumpur (ISKL), as they were increasing their inclusive efforts. As we worked through the idea of selecting a time in the day for what we'd often seen called WIN Time (what I need time) or flex block, it was clear that the seventh grade team wanted to charge forward with this. But it was the middle of the academic year, and changing the master schedule was not an option at that time. There were four sections in the seventh grade class, but as is always the case, each grouping of seventh graders were in different subjects at any given point in the day. But without changing the master schedule, they were able to coordinate the small group instruction in just those four classrooms.

We decided that during the day, the four teachers would agree on what time small-group instruction would be. They didn't have to agree on what was being taught during their whole-group time, and they didn't have to agree on how they were teaching. They only had to agree on the time frame for coordinated small-group instruction. During the coordinated small-group instruction time, each teacher planned several small groups. Some of those may be related to the lesson they were teaching at the moment, and others were small groups for intervention or support. A student who was in the language arts class may have needed math intervention, and during this small-group time, the student could go to the group where this support was given. What a beautiful way to allow students to make choice and differentiate for themselves! The seventh grade team at ISKL had such success with coordinating their small-group instruction that the practice grew throughout the school, and the teachers now support other schools wanting to implement it.

For students who needed ongoing intervention, they were able to get real intervention for as long as they needed and move out of the intervention group when they no longer did. Some of the small groups had teachers, and others were independent. Specialists were able to lead a small group intervention across four classes, and not one student was pulled from core instruction. For this to be true, all four teachers had to agree that during coordinated small-group instruction, *no new content could be delivered.* This was a time to practice, receive support, extend, and differentiate. Any of the groups can be anywhere in the building, and being in a small space outside the classroom does not imply special education. This is a good reason not to have any small spaces labeled "special education" or "resource" room. Small spaces can be used for a variety of reasons! There are many times groups may want or need a smaller or quieter space for learning. Intervention is only one possibility.

COORDINATED SMALL-GROUP INSTRUCTION

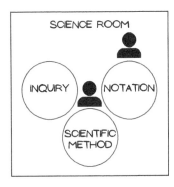
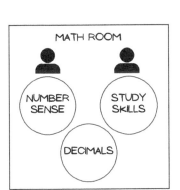

As you can see from the illustrated example, some of the groups had a teacher or specialist, and others involved an independent activity. Some of the teachers may "float" between two groups. Some of the groups were for intervention, and others were not. Some of the intervention groups are within the larger classroom, and others are in small spaces. Some of the smaller spaces were not for intervention. For students who need targeted intervention, or tier two intervention, they can be a part of the intervention group 2–3 days per week. For those who need intensive, or a tier three level of intervention, they can take part in the intervention group every day.

One lesson I've learned since this time in working with other schools is that we can bring a lot of efficiency to this by staggering the small-group instruction throughout the day. So, second grade, for example, can do this at 10:00, third grade at 11:00, and fourth grade at 12:00. By staggering like this, specialists can now deliver intervention in small groups without pulling from core instruction several times during the day across grade levels. Staggering does create a "spreadsheet challenge," but building leaders are masterful at the schedule and, no doubt, might be the ones to effectively lead the solution in some schools. And really, this spreadsheet challenge is less than the challenge specialists face when trying to meet the needs of students who need support but are dispersed.

CASE STORY

Ms. Talbert joined her PLC group with the agenda of planning the coordinated small group instruction for the next six weeks. The group included four classroom teachers, an ELL teacher, two special educators, a reading specialist, and two counselors. The group meets on a regular basis and each six weeks the agenda is to think about what skills the students across the grade need the most. After efficient discussion, led by Mx. Brackenstein using an activity to bring consensus, they determined fifteen priorities for the next six-week small-group rotation:

I. Writing Clarity	6. Time Management	II. Number Sense
2. Decimals	7. Number Sense	12. Emotional Regulation
3. Inquiry and Curiosity	8. Scientific Notation	13. Scientific Method
4. Note Taking	9. Evaluating Sources	14. Conflict Resolution
5. Tech Project	10. Independent Reading	15. Reading Fluency

Next, the group decided which teachers would be responsible for which groups and where those groups will occur. Ms. Talbert chose the groups for time management, quiet reading, and writing clarity. She planned to lead the group on time-management, with Mx. Brackenstein leading the group on writing clarity. As they thought about which students might participate in each group, there were both students with and without labels who needed each of these skills.

One caution about coordinated small-group learning: this should not be "intervention or enrichment block." This should not be the time of day where if you are having a hard time with something you go for help, and everyone else gets to do something fun. This also should not be "intervention or study hall" time, in which there is nothing planned unless you receive an intervention. *Everyone* has a need. Even the "straight-A" student has a need. This is a time when all instruction stops, and students go to the spaces and teachers they need to go to have these needs met. During this pause, there can be a space for a specific math intervention, an English language support, a reading intervention, a counseling session, and any other priority teachers identify. These priorities should be revisited every 6 to 8 weeks to determine if group targets should change. Teams should also review data during this time to see when students need to move in or out of any intervention. Giving students options for where they work and what they work gives students the autonomy they need. And we facilitate self-regulation when we help students revisit goals they set to celebrate success and coach them to determine their next priorities. For students who are required to receive an intervention during this time, teachers should incorporate many other kinds of choices within that intervention time.

REFLECTION

How do you see coordinated small-group learning working at your school? What are the existing structures and systems in place that could allow for the use of this logistical solution? What are the barriers to a shift to this service delivery model?

(Continued)

(Continued)

_____

_____

_____

_____

_____

SUMMARY

Even with the best universally accessible and inclusive design, some students are still going to require support or intervention. Intervention means so much more than adding a paraprofessional or helping students with assignments. It means systematically supporting a student to mastery on a critical skill using research-based practices.

1. Any student who needs intervention should get it,

2. They need real intervention,

3. Students should not be pulled from core instruction to receive intervention,

4. Small-group instruction works, and

5. Students should start and stop intervention as they need it.

In order to provide students with the ongoing, flexible support they need, we don't need to have labels or even special spaces devoted to provide this support. These spaces with labels attached to them isolate students and often limit who can receive intervention. Alternatives like coordinated small-group learning offer options for every student to get what they need, as much as they need, and only for as long as they need.

SELF-ASSESSMENT

I can describe three "nonnegotiables" of MTSS and compare and contrast those to the practices of my school.

① ② ③ ④ ⑤

I can articulate the harmful effects of one-to-one paraprofessional roles and design alternatives that work.

① ② ③ ④ ⑤

I can compare and contrast the definition of intervention to how support is provided in my school.

① ② ③ ④ ⑤

I can apply coordinated small-group instruction by designing a schedule for delivering flexible, responsive intervention across classrooms.

① ② ③ ④ ⑤

CHAPTER SEVEN

Mastery Assessment and Grading

Assessment, Feedback, and Grades Are a GPS to Facilitate Learning

AFTER DITCHING A FOCUS ON POINTS AND PERCENTAGES, MS. TALBERT'S STUDENTS FINALLY HAD A GPS TO REACH THEIR GOALS.

Learning Intentions	Success Criteria
I am learning about the barriers introduced by many traditional grading practices.	I can describe how my students are performing without percentages, averaging, zeros, or a focus on points.
I am learning about the relative roles of assessment, grading, and feedback to guide student mastery.	I can describe the roles of assessment, feedback, and grades, using a GPS metaphor.
I am learning about formative and summative use of assessment information.	I can explain the difference between formative and summative uses of information and distinguish this from the formality of assessment.
I am learning about goal attainment scales that support multiple means of expression.	I can develop a "task-agnostic" goal attainment scale for a current standard I am teaching.
I am learning about how to grade students on skills and understandings instead of tasks.	I can determine a final grade, using rules of logic instead of points, percentages, and averages.

No discussion of classroom equity is complete without consideration of assessment and grades. Although it may feel like students need to have grades to be motivated, decades of research has taught us that feedback is most effective in the absence of a grade (e.g., Black & Wiliam, 1998; Butler & Nisan, 1986; Butler, 1988; Dweck, 2000; Elawar & Corno, 1985; Lipnevich & Smith, 2009). Grades do not improve performance, and there is evidence to show they are detrimental. It may feel counterintuitive, but any motivation we see from adding grades is purely extrinsic and may actually disrupt learning. Safe environments foster collaboration, not the competition that is inherent in traditional grading practices.

A GPS FOR LEARNING

When is the last time you remember navigating to a new place in your car without the aid of a global positioning system? Most of us can't imagine driving to a new city or perhaps even within our own cities without the technology of our smart phones or GPS systems in our cars. At our fingertips we are able to see clearly our desired destination, our current location, and precise directions for how to get where we are going. And each of these components, the destination, location, and directions, reported to us in real time, work together to get where we want to be.

The way that we plan curriculum, assign grades, and provide students with meaningful feedback should work together to provide a powerful educational GPS to guide student success. We can think of the components of the educational GPS in this way: The success criteria are the destination, the feedback is the turn-by-turn directions that guide learning, and the grade is the current location.

Destination: Where Am I Going?

The first step to using any GPS is identifying the destination. No other piece of the GPS has any meaning without a desired destination. For students, the success criteria, standards, and effective approaches to learning are the destination. This is where we are going with this lesson, group of lessons, or by the end of the year. Knowing where they are going is a prerequisite for students' taking in feedback and adjusting their steps in learning. As presented in Chapter 4 on engagement, support-ing students to have a full understanding of the destination involves more than including standards or success criteria in our learning management software or posting them in the classroom. We have to dialogue with students to ensure they understand where they are going. They should know how it will look and feel when they arrive. Students should be able to state in their own words the success criteria for both standards and approaches to learning. They've got it when they can connect the learning intentions and success criteria across content and time as a journey to the standards. This dialogue on learning intentions and success criteria may seem like it could take away from the precious time needed to teach the content, but it should be seen, instead, as an investment and an integral part of the teaching.

In addition to the academic success criteria, by guiding students to set their own learning intentions and success criteria for the process of learning, we set them up to be self-regulated adults who know who they are as learners and have personalized strategies to succeed. Students' approaches to their learning are transferable to numerous contexts and include skills such as students' meta-cognition, persistence, conflict resolution, compassion, written and spoken communication, problem-solving, organization of space and materials, studying, and the like. The way a student approaches to learning are often far more important than the content of the lesson we are teaching. But this is a contrast to the way many of us were educated. When you were in school, did your teachers focus on your knowledge of facts and procedures? Was this what was graded? Was it common to learn something long enough to get through a test. Or did your teachers use lessons and learning experiences to actively teach and provide feedback on transferable, process skills? If it was the latter, you are fortunate!

REFLECTION

Academic success isn't the only destination we have for our students. Students' names appear on honor rolls and class ranking lists to reward those with the highest academic grades. We celebrate academic achievement at graduation and award ceremonies. These academic grades are front and center of electronic gradebooks that not only students access but also their families—sometimes daily. But ask any educator what makes a great student, and you'll likely hear the words: engaged, curious, kind, gives effort, motivated, organized, globally minded, critical thinker, compassionate, works well with others, communicates well, and uses metacognition skills. These are skills and qualities every student (and adult) in the building is working to improve. And, if you think about it, these are probably more important than the content we teach. We can't teach these skills and strategies without content, but in some ways the content is merely a vehicle for these qualities we value most. How are we including these values prominently within our teaching and assessment as a valued "destination?"

_____

_____

_____

_____

_____

Turn-by-Turn Directions: How Do I Get There?

Without a doubt, the most important function your GPS provides is to give you the directions to get where you are going. You need to know where you're going, and having your location helps you to make decisions, but we all know that what keeps us from getting lost and frustrated are those turn-by-turn directions.

For students, the turn-by-turn directions are the carefully crafted and well-timed feedback situated within formative assessment practices that helps students navigate the curriculum. Students perform better, and are less anxious and more focused, when they receive personal feedback that is detailed, clearly shows the gap between where they are now and where they are going, and shows teacher confidence that they can achieve the expectation. Feedback is a powerful intervention (feedback: $d = .62$). Thus, the turn-by-turn directions offered by feedback are the cornerstone of our assessment practices. And, if we are primarily using our classroom assessments to guide our instruction, then, by definition, we are primarily using our classroom assessments formatively.

FEEDBACK

-1.00   0.0   1.50

Location: Where Am I Now?

As you make your way to your desired destination, your GPS gives you information on where you are and how far this is from your destination. As you look to the moving dot or arrow on your GPS, you expect this information to be accurate, and up to the second. This is the only function that scores on assignments or grades should serve. The GPS does not average your location over time because the only useful information about location is where you are *right now*. And as important as the scoring task can feel to a teacher (and to students), the only information that a score is able to give is current location. So, it had better serve that function well! Like the moving arrow on your phone's map or in a GPS, that score tells the students where they are *right now* toward the destination. Before we ever talk about *how* to assess and grade in ways that support equity and growth, we need to first ask, for each learning experience and task, "Is it necessary and helpful to give a score or grade?" **If it isn't necessary *and* helpful, don't do it**.

Grading as a Barrier

Think back to the beginning of this book and the discussion around internal locus of control (believing you have control over what happens to you) and self-efficacy (believing you have what it takes to make that happen). Now, imagine you are really struggling, for whatever reason, with your understanding of a concept in school. Chances are, you can reach back in your memory for just such an example. Now, imagine that you struggled with this for the first half of the year, falling way behind your peers and far behind the expectation at that time. But, you worked really hard, and your teacher worked really hard, too, and with much effort on both of your parts, you did it! You reached the expectation by the end of the year. Well, if your teacher used an average across time to determine your grade, you were lucky to receive a C.

Not all grading practices are created equal. Many commonly used grading practices introduce barriers to a culture of inclusion and mastery in our classrooms. Without a safe grading culture established, grades will continue to be seen as something students earn and *who* they are, rather than a reflection of their learning and *where* they are. And without this culture of mastery, we breed competition instead of collaboration, and a "one size fits all" view of success. For students in our classes who need the most academic support to succeed, what could be more harmful to a student's self-efficacy and locus of control than a culture of competitive grading. And students who are already marginalized in some way take the brunt of that hit. Grading can take the student who needs the most support and introduce even more barriers than they are already experiencing. If we must assign a score or grade, we need to first do so without causing harm, and the following practices do just that. They subvert our ability to tell students where they are in their progress toward success criteria.

Averaging Grades. For students who quickly grasp the material we teach, or even come into our classes already understanding the content, the harm of the average isn't readily apparent. But for students who take longer or require more support or intervention to achieve the expectation, nothing is more defeating than being held hostage to an average. Averaging immediately amplifies inequities that already exist in our student population. We all reflected at the beginning of this book how we want to "make a difference" as educators. The average completely disregards the difference we make.

Let's consider three students: Chris, Spencer, and Maisie. Chris mastered the standard early on and maintained that performance. Spencer made steady progress and mastered the standard in the end. Maisie really struggled for a long time, but in the end, she, too, mastered the standard. If we average their scores, Chris ends up with a much higher score than Spencer, and Maisie receives the lowest score. But they all got there! Shouldn't Maisie also receive the high score? Shouldn't the teacher receive the high score for Maisie? Maisie's performance, in fact, shows that teacher's effectiveness better than the others. Chris came in with a high level of existing skills on this standard. His performance is not evidence of good teaching. He probably would have performed well even with poor teaching. It's Maisie's performance that is the evidence of good teaching. To average grades across a reporting period is like saying, "I don't care if my teaching has any effect on student learning." We hope students improve during the reporting period as a result of our excellent teaching and feedback!

With this averaged grade, Maisie's teacher is telling her no matter how hard she works, if she didn't walk into this class with the ability to catch on quickly, she can never achieve to the same level as the students who did. Her disadvantage in understanding quickly also disadvantages her in the grading process—even if she achieves at the same level as her peers in the end. There is no compelling reason to average grades, and plenty of research to the contrary. On the other hand, when grades are centered on *current performance* students have reason to keep trying. And it's not only the students who deserve grades based on most recent performance—teachers also deserve credit for their accomplishments to get students there!

Percentage Grades. Another way we can ensure the clarity of the grade in communicating current location is to use scales that are appropriate for the information on learning that we have. Percentage grades are among the most frequently used but are rarely an accurate way to indicate level of learning. Although debates of logic and philosophy with regard to grading can be interesting, this issue of percentage grades is not a question of philosophy—it's one of sound measurement. Percentages are typically calculated by determining the percentage of items correct. But what does that tell us about level of proficiency toward a standard? We are not able, for example, to say that a student has attained 93% of the standard. Saying that a student got 93% of items correct is not the same as the student has 93% of the success criteria. It only says they got 93% of items correct.

Assigning percentage to a learning product *feels* objective because we have calculated something. But what is behind that calculation is more arbitrary than using our professional judgment as educators to summarize a student's learning. Percentage of items correct is based on the items I select, the level of difficulty I determined, the mode of responses I expect, and what I'll count for partial or full credit. I had complete control over the task! This is why a 93% with an "easy teacher" may actually not be as much of an accomplishment as an 83% with a "difficult teacher." The idea that percentages are somehow infallible because there is math involved is nothing short of smoke and mirrors. Because a clear understanding of where students are in their gaining of skills and understandings is fundamental to our ability to target the needs of individual students, not having this understanding harms the students who need support the most.

I remember a time when my oldest child failed the end of course exam for algebra. He received a score below 70% on the exam and, because of this, was required to take the course again. This overly simple view of success, needs, and the intervention required ignored the skills and understandings *within* algebra that were needed. To simply repeat the course is like saying, "Well, it didn't work the first time, but let's do it again anyway." A percentage score is rarely the best way to make visible the specific areas of strength and need for a student. As the team and I reviewed my child's math exam, it became clear he made only one type of error: he mixed up positive and negative signs, causing him to arrive at the wrong answers.

My child is now a college graduate with a degree in mathematics—he's a "math guy" and was a "math kid." He had excellent conceptual understanding and procedural understanding, but his precision with the details was his need. He didn't need to repeat the course—he needed support on attending to these details that we often incorrectly label "careless errors." But by reducing algebra skills and understandings to percentage of items correct, we are unable to tell the difference between a student who has a need in the area of precision versus one who has a need in conceptual understanding. Without this clear understanding, we can't respond just in time with the right strategies or intervention. And isn't this the main purpose of classroom assessment: to guide instruction and intervention?

Zeros. You may have never neglected to do an assignment or forgot to turn one in, but most of us have. And what was the resulting consequence—for most of us, it was a zero. This traditional practice is aimed at punishing students for irresponsibility by lowering their academic grade. But a need to support self-regulation, organization, or responsibility is very different from the need to support academic learning. Mixing the two is a recipe for failing our students. When we combine criteria for learning with students' approaches to learning or behaviors, we take away the ability to communicate about each of these and, more importantly, to respond to these very different needs.

For the student who is not turning in work, this could be because they didn't understand the work but don't have the advocacy skills to ask for help. One student could be having difficulty with relationships at home or with friends. Another may be experiencing trauma that you will never know about. There may be significant responsibilities at home for the student. The student could experience depression or anxiety that pose barriers. Another might be coming to terms with gender identity or sexual orientation. One may be bullied for being different. Another student may feel they shouldn't even bother because they can't succeed. The student may not have the tools or strategies to be organized or to persist with difficult work. And the list goes on. The point is, a zero cannot be a proxy for missing work. Missing work is not the same as evidence of no learning. Missing work is just that—missing. And the reason for this needs to be understood so we can respond, teach, and support appropriately.

Combining Compliance Grades With Learning Grades. Many classrooms continue to have policies that wield grades as punishment for behaviors such as late work, participation, or challenging behaviors. When grades are used to punish behavior, the true meaning of the grade becomes unclear. A student, for example, who receives a "C" may have learned the content well but failed to submit homework or submitted assignments late. Or the student may have demonstrated compliant behavior but failed to master the content. When indicators of behavior and achievement are combined in this way, we can no longer tell the difference.

Not only does including indicators of compliance or participation in an achievement grade cause difficulties with interpreting the grade, but this practice is also harmful to students' motivation and engagement. When grades are lowered because of late work or missing homework, especially if the penalties are severe, students can lose hope that they can achieve, damaging their motivation to try. Students who submit work late need more than our recording of their lateness; they need our support. Some students may have difficulty with executive functioning and *want* to be punctual. Others may have low self-efficacy and have lost motivation to be engaged in the content—or school in general. Still others may have enormous responsibilities at home and don't have enough time or support to do homework. Before we can address any pattern of late work, we must understand why it's happening. Time and project management are self-regulation skills to be learned, not inherent character traits. Our job, then, is to use practices to support students, academically and emotionally. Grades are not the way to do this.

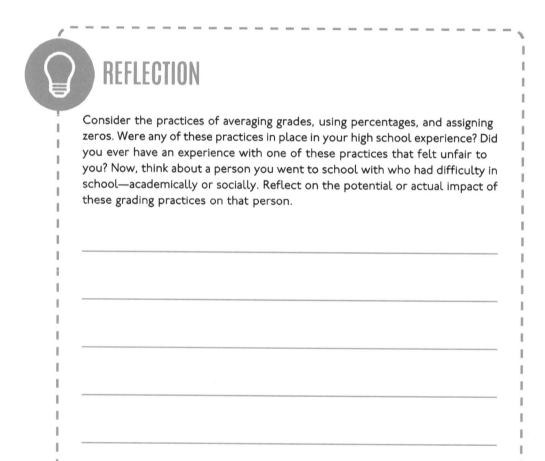

REFLECTION

Consider the practices of averaging grades, using percentages, and assigning zeros. Were any of these practices in place in your high school experience? Did you ever have an experience with one of these practices that felt unfair to you? Now, think about a person you went to school with who had difficulty in school—academically or socially. Reflect on the potential or actual impact of these grading practices on that person.

_____

_____

_____

_____

_____

ASSESSMENT FOR LEARNING

While most people generally use the term "formative" to mean the task is for practice and will be used to inform instruction and learning, there seems to also be an interpretation that formative tasks are informal, and summative tasks are formal.

But categorizing *the type* of tasks and activities as formative or summative is a harmful misuse of the terms. Formative and summative are terms we use to describe *how we use* the information from the assessment (Black, 2013). The notion of formality has *nothing* to do with whether a task is formative or summative.

If formative assessment is designed to open "opportunities for using that evidence to develop a learning dialogue" (Black, 2013, p. 169), then students benefit when all of our assessments are used formatively, until the opportunity for learning is over (formative assessment: $d = .40$). So, we don't really have formative tasks and summative tasks. We have a formative period of time and summative points in time. The formative period of time happens the entire school year, and is focused on building mastery, with only a small portion of the year being spent on summative assessment, and mostly at the end.

The implications for this shift mean that every test, activity, check-in, paper, and project is, in fact, used formatively until the end of the year (even if we pause to use some of this evidence summatively at reporting periods). And every bit of information, formal or informal, is considered an important data point that we can use to summarize learning at the end. This gets us out of the game of categorizing what "counts," because it *all* counts.

Using data summatively—that is, to summarize learning—should only happen when we need to report learning, typically at the end of reporting periods. Those grades should only become "fixed" at the end of the academic year. With this mindset, we don't really have to have formative tasks and summative tasks. We can have a formative period of time and summative points in time. The formative period happens over the entire school year, with only a small portion of the year, mostly at the end of terms, spent on summative assessment.

This approach also prevents us from only including formal tests and final exams or projects in the final grade. At the end of the academic year, we have the task of summarizing where

each student is on a set of standards, proficiencies, or competencies. Have you ever taught a student who you knew
understood the content and had the skills down but who
performed poorly on the big test or project? When we see
summative as a point in time rather than a type of task, we are
free to use all types of evidence, formal and informal, to make a
decision on how to summarize where a student is. If we know
the student understands, but they demonstrated their understanding better informally than on the test, then the test
wasn't a good measure of that student's understanding.

FORMATIVE ASSESSMENT

d = .40

-1.00	0.0	1.50

The opportunity for assessments to be used formatively is
completely lost without feedback. But well-intended feedback
isn't always effective. Feedback is only effective if students
actually use it! To that end, feedback needs to be specific
about the next steps, encouraging, actionable, and delivered
as soon as possible (Wiliam, 2016). We also have to devote
time *in class* for students to spend time reflecting on and
using the feedback to chart a course forward. We are most
effective when we teach students not only to revise a product
to improve it but how to improve their transferable skills.
When we can see evidence of student improvement across
multiple tasks and performances, we know our feedback was
effective.

SCALES OF PROGRESS

In Chapter 3, we thought about the importance of giving
students multiple options for how they show what they know,
can do, and understand. Remember the discussion in that
chapter on tasks versus skills and understandings? The skills
and understandings are what we really care about, and the
tasks are only the ways we measure. We have many options
for tasks, as you discovered in the maps you created for
multiple means of expression. Let's look at Ms. Talbert's
map again.

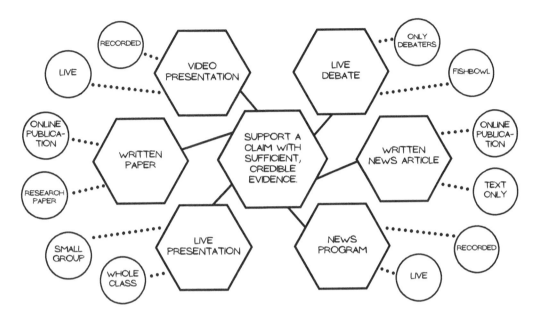

You may be thinking that the idea of giving students multiple options for showing what they understand and can do is a great idea. But having a rubric for each of the options may seem daunting, especially if using points, averages, and percentages can be harmful. The task of creating separate rubrics for each of the options of expression can feel overwhelming. Fortunately, the task of creating measures becomes simpler and less time-consuming within a UDL approach in which scales are centered on skills and understandings instead of tasks. To this end, we essentially develop "task-agnostic" scales instead of task-specific rubrics. These scales, as with any learning progression, can be applied to any type of task that a student chooses.

If Ms. Talbert had the job of creating a rubric for each one of these options for expression, she'd never have time to teach! Fortunately, she only needs to develop *one* scale: the one for supporting a claim with sufficient, credible evidence. In this scale, the descriptors can only be about this skill and have no reference to specific tasks, like speaking or writing. The scale should be applicable to any of the options for expression. Unlike in a rubric, the first point on the scale doesn't describe what's wrong or bad about the student's learning. It is only a location on the path to the goal, or standard.

This type of measurement is based on learning progression work and on goal attainment scaling, which has its roots in social work and medicine. Goal attainment scales were designed as a way to measure progress on a skill selected for a single person. Goal attainment scales can be thought of as a ruler of sorts—one that allows us to measure progress in many ways. All too often, measures of learning are limited to calculating a percentage. But most skills neither should be—or can be—measured using a percentage. By applying the concept of goal attainment scaling to our classroom assessments, we use whatever metric of measurement that makes sense for a standard or goal. If a student wants to persist in his reading longer, then duration measured in minutes may be best. If a student wants to complete a certain type of task with less help, then level of independence may be the right measure. Or, if we want the quality of a skill to progress, we can use words to describe the characteristics of each step in the progression. For example, it may be more meaningful (and easier) to describe the level of support a student needs to edit writing for accurate spelling, grammar, and punctuation than to attempt to measure a percentage of accuracy with these skills.

SELF-REFLECTION

$d = .75$

-1.00   0.0   1.50

I've taught this type of goal setting with a scale to many groups of students. Walking through a collaborative peer-to-peer goal-setting process, students develop meaningful personal goals, strategies to put into place, and a goal attainment scale as the ruler. With any of our classroom assessments, determining progress should be something we do with students, not to them. Engaging students in self-reflection of their own progress relative to a goal develops their skills in self-regulation and metacognition. Self-reflection is an effective influence, then, not only in the short term and situated within a class or unit, (self-reflection: $d = .75$) but also a metacognitive skill needed throughout life. Goal attainment scaling is another tool we can give students to build metacognitive skills in self-monitoring.

CASE STORY

Rather than a rubric for each task, Ms. Talbert developed a goal attainment scale to assess students' learning throughout the year. At first, this seemed to be more time consuming, because she had to think through exactly how students would progress in their learning over the year. She reframed her thinking about the "bottom" of the scale. Normally, in her rubrics, the bottom (or left) of the rubric included what was missing or wrong. But in developing a goal attainment scale, she simply described the learning progression toward the end-of-year success criteria for the standard.

For Ms. Talbert's success criteria for supporting a claim with evidence, it made the most sense to her to describe the qualities of this skill over time. Each of the points along the way represented success criteria that built throughout the year. With no references to the specific task, the scale could be used with any task. Better, Ms. Talbert's students used the scale to assess and dialogue about their own learning throughout the year.

STEP	SKILL: SUPPORT A CLAIM WITH SUFFICIENT, CREDIBLE EVIDENCE
5	I can synthesize information from multiple sources to make connections, highlight patterns in the information, draw conclusions, and reconcile any conflicting evidence or information.
4	I can analyze credible information from multiple sources to reveal similarities and differences in the evidence, information, and existing positions.
3	I can use multiple criteria for evaluating the credibility of information (such as authority of source, age of information, quality of the evidence, amount of evidence, and convergence of information).
2	I can use 1–2 criteria for evaluating the credibility of information (such as authority of source).
1	I can take information from multiple sources and selects the information that is most relevant to the question being answered or position being taken.

ACTION

To create a goal attainment scale for a learning intention you have this year, first select a skill that is critically important—a skill students will need for a lifetime and across many tasks in school and in life. Although you can create a goal attainment scale for any skill, it's a good idea to prioritize and start with the most important. Sometimes these skills are ones that come from the standards, but you can also choose one that is a transferrable approach to learning.

Once you choose the skill, the first step is to describe the starting point for the year in observable terms. This starting point is based on where students are at the beginning of the academic year. Try to phrase this in terms of what students do instead of what they don't do. Next, determine the end-of-year success criteria—setting the bar high—and describe this top level. Finally, pick intermediary points and describe these. You may end up using numbers in your success criteria, but you also may not. There are no rules. Pick the descriptions that make the most sense, are easy to observe and apply to many contexts, and use student-friendly words.

STEP	SKILL: SUPPORT A CLAIM WITH SUFFICIENT, CREDIBLE EVIDENCE
5	
4	
3	
2	
1	

ASSESSMENT OF LEARNING

Using data summatively, to summarize learning (Black, 2013), happens when we need to report learning—typically at the end of reporting periods, and those grades should only become "fixed" at the end of the academic year. That is, it isn't until the end of the year (or course) that the function of the assessment is only summative. This means that during the academic year, even when we are using information to report summatively, this information should also be serving the purpose of informing instruction and learning. The implications for this shift mean that every test, activity, check-in, paper, project, is, in fact, used formatively until the end of the year (even if we pause to use some of this evidence summatively at reporting periods).

Understanding that summative grading isn't necessarily formal also prevents us from only having to include formal tests and final exams or projects in the final grade. At the end of the academic year, we have the task of summarizing where each student is on a set of standards, proficiencies, or competencies. When we see summative as a point in time rather than a type of task, we are free to use all types of evidence, formal and informal, to make a decision on how to summarize where a student is. Sometimes the best and most valid assessment of a student's learning comes from an informal, warm conversation with a student about their work.

Have you ever taught a student who you were positive understood the content and had the skills but performed poorly on the big test or project at the end? If we know the student understands but they demonstrated their understanding better informally than on the test, then the test wasn't a good measure of that student's understanding. If we want students to stop asking if work "counts," then we have to use the terms "formative" and "summative" correctly. Every bit of information, formal or informal, is an important data point that we use to summarize learning at the end. Teaching students the meanings of formative and summative gets us out of the game of categorizing what "counts," because it all

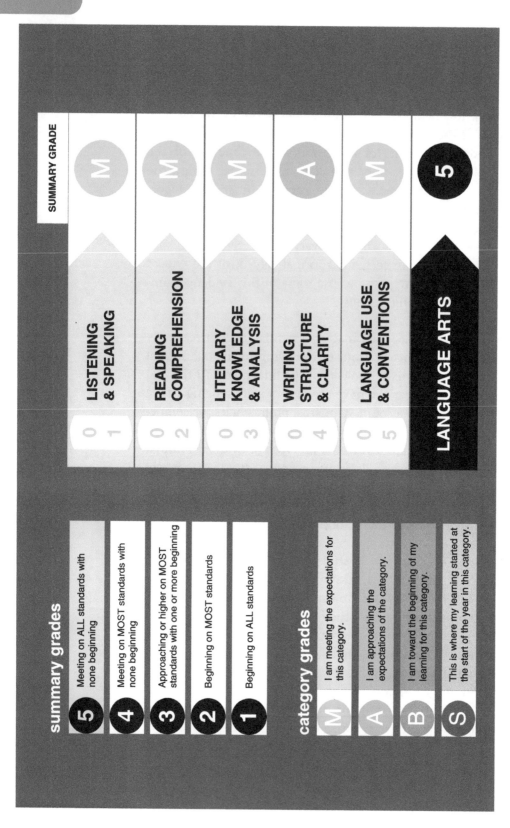

SUMMARY GRADE

	SUMMARY GRADE
01 LISTENING & SPEAKING	M
02 READING COMPREHENSION	M
03 LITERARY KNOWLEDGE & ANALYSIS	M
04 WRITING STRUCTURE & CLARITY	A
05 LANGUAGE USE & CONVENTIONS	M
LANGUAGE ARTS	5

summary grades

5 Meeting on ALL standards with none beginning

4 Meeting on MOST standards with none beginning

3 Approaching or higher on MOST standards with one or more beginning

2 Beginning on MOST standards

1 Beginning on ALL standards

category grades

M I am meeting the expectations for this category.

A I am approaching the expectations of the category.

B I am toward the beginning of my learning for this category.

S This is where my learning started at the start of the year in this category.

counts. And although everything counts, it isn't fixed as a grade until the end—the final location.

Determining the final grade is far from the most important function of grades, but the fact remains that most teachers are still required to assign grades at minimum at the end of each reporting period. When students have engaged in reflecting on their progress throughout the year, they continue and con-ference again with their teacher to co-reflect at the end of the year. This self-determining of grades, then, is not a separate, new, or anxiety-producing event; it's simply the last time during the academic year they reflect on their learning with their teacher. And this process, over time, improves student success (self-reported grades: $d = 1.33$).

SELF-REPORTED GRADES

d=1.33

-1.00   0.0   1.50

When it comes time to assign a symbol for the final grade, rather than using the harmful grading practices from earlier in this chapter, rules of logic are the best bet for equity *and* accu-racy. With rules of logic, we attach qualitative meaning to cat-egories and make informed judgments based on rules for using these categories, rather than using calculations. Computers use only numbers. They know nothing of the individual students, the learning environment, how the student progressed over time, and are more likely to harm marginalized students or those disadvantaged by harmful grading practices.

CASE STORY

The end of the year was upon them, and with that, came Ms. Talbert's requirement for summative assessment of students' learning. She had always administered a written exam for this requirement. But her internal conflict began to grow as she realized this written exam would absolutely not show about half of her students' best work. But could she give options on a final the same way she did throughout the year on formative assessments? She decided to give it a try but was a little nervous.

(Continued)

(Continued)

Ms. Talbert engaged her students in dialogue about how they each grew in their ability to support a claim in different ways over the year. Individually, the students conferenced with her to reflect on their personal goals for the semester and revisit how confident they used to be in presenting their views through speaking, writing, multimedia, and in front of small and large groups. Some of her students were surprised reading their reflections and reviewing their goal attainment scales from the beginning of the year. They'd forgotten that certain ways of expression were difficult before! After conferencing with each student, Ms. Talbert gave students the option to publish an online blog and engage with readers on a topic of their choice, to present in front of the class, or to present with a smaller group, entertaining questions from the group and responding. The requirements for the skill were the same, regardless of which way students chose to express their understanding and skills.

For the grades she assigned at the end of the year, the summative point in time, Ms. Talbert again conferenced with each student, and suggest their own grade. She gave students a chance to describe their learning and determine the grade with her, reviewing their work. While she was doing this with each student, other students were providing feedback to one another on their final assessments, grouped by the task they chose.

Ms. Talbert used "rules of logic," rather than mathematical operations to determine options for the final grade. In her school, Ms. Talbert had to report a traditional grade: A, B, C, D, or E. In Ms. Talbert's school, report cards included power standards, and her goal attainment scales were calibrated to these standards, with specific success criteria. She used the five points on her goal attainment scale as she conferenced with students, with each description on the scale being recorded as a letter on the report card. She did not use these letters until the end, even though students knew that it would be communicated this way in the end. But students always knew exactly where they were toward the end-of-year expectation and could clearly describe their destination, current location, and the next steps in their learning journey.

SUMMARY

By having a solid grasp on the role of formative assessment, feedback, and a role of mentorship in our classroom assessment practices, we open the door to give all students the same opportunity for success. Significant barriers for students persist in the form of grading practices that have been used in education for over a century. Practices such as averaging, calculating percentages, and giving zeros for missing work are invalid ways of measuring or communicating learning. Worse, these practices are inequitable, causing disadvantage mostly to students who have needs for support. Students who need intervention or take longer to master expectations are disproportionately harmed by averaging. Percentage grades give us little to no information on what needs a student actually has. And assigning zeros for missing work, rather than providing the support they need to be able to complete and submit work, instead achieves the opposite in harming students' self-efficacy. When we establish group norms, model a "mentorship" role, and shift our assessment and grading practices, we teach our students that all students can succeed, we *expect* them to do so, and we will work as a team to get everyone there.

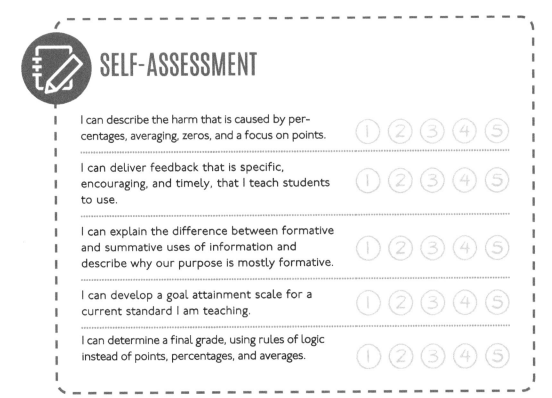

SELF-ASSESSMENT

I can describe the harm that is caused by percentages, averaging, zeros, and a focus on points. ① ② ③ ④ ⑤

I can deliver feedback that is specific, encouraging, and timely, that I teach students to use. ① ② ③ ④ ⑤

I can explain the difference between formative and summative uses of information and describe why our purpose is mostly formative. ① ② ③ ④ ⑤

I can develop a goal attainment scale for a current standard I am teaching. ① ② ③ ④ ⑤

I can determine a final grade, using rules of logic instead of points, percentages, and averages. ① ② ③ ④ ⑤

CHAPTER EIGHT

Looking Forward

Build Teams That Are Interdisciplinary "Machines" for Equity and Inclusion

Learning Intentions	Success Criteria
I am learning about the value of a whole-school approach to implementing universal design for the learning (UDL).	I can reflect on the initiatives my school has taken on in recent years and identify patterns of these initiatives that "stuck."
I am learning about nested levels of school change.	I can use Dilt's nested levels of logic to reflect on where my school is to determine my needs and the needs of my school.
I am learning about how we can support one another as adults to build whole-school capacity.	I can facilitate discussion and decision-making around the type of support that adults need, including my own, to carry out UDL and intervention.

The many influences that make up a universal design for learning (UDL) approach have the potential to make an enormous impact on students. The strategies in this book are not an exhaustive list, but rather offer a starting point for making decisions on how to continuously evaluate and improve our instruction. In building capacity within an organization, I'd be remiss to omit the equity issues we *do not* have control over. As much work as we do on supporting schools to be more inclusive, there are barriers that remain in the educational system. Schools are funded based on property taxes, with the wealthiest districts having the greatest resources. Schools that are higher poverty have a greater challenge, but also a more pressing need, to support their students' basic needs and learning within their context. But the instructional design work we can do to make our schools more equitable *does* make a difference.

WHOLE SCHOOL IMPROVEMENT PROGRAMS

d=.33

-1.00   0.0   1.50

Although any group of students can benefit from more UDL in their class-rooms, the real power comes from a whole school taking on the priority (whole school programs: $d = .33$). UDL is not a new initiative, but rather a framework for organizing time-tested strategies around student engagement, comprehension, and expression of their learning. When whole schools coordinate a unified effort, the outcomes for students skyrocket. Whole-school efforts sometimes do not allow for a lot of teacher choice and options to differentiate their learning. (In other words, whole-school initiatives and the corresponding professional development all too often are not universally designed.) But a push for equitable and inclusive design in every classroom is different. The UDL framework offers numerous next steps, from the person who is new to the idea, all the way to people who have been studying this for years. I definitely have my next steps—even as a teacher of adults. UDL pushes us to think critically about students' learning within our lesson design to make each lesson effective for more students, especially those who need support the most. The goal is not to use every strategy in every lesson, but rather to think critically about our content and how we can remove the barriers, the confounding variables.

REFLECTION

Reflect back to the landscape of UDL strategies. What do you see as your personal priorities? Dialogue with a small group of your colleagues. What are their priorities for what to take on next?

_____

_____

_____

_____

_____

Enough of the pep rally on why schools should take on the challenge. *How* does a school coordinate its efforts to enable and expedite teacher's use of ever-increasing inclusive design? In order to answer that question, let's take a look at a nested view of school change (adapted from Dilts levels of logic: Ehmer, 2018) to consider the ways schools can implement equitable and inclusive efforts. In this model, there are six levels of organizational change, and each one depends on the ones below it—thus, they are "nested," much like a set of nested mixing bowls or toy nesting cups for young children. Each level has to be large enough and have enough capacity for the next level to fit.

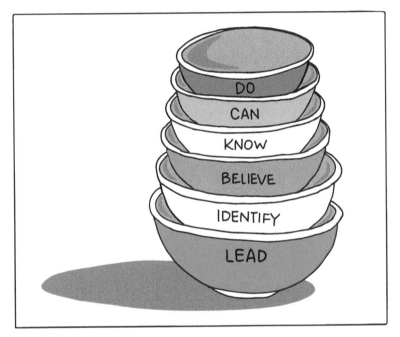

DO
CAN
KNOW
BELIEVE
IDENTIFY
LEAD

NESTED LEVELS OF CHANGE

DO

The simplest part of a school's efforts to be more inclusive is to simply not default to segregating students by the groups to which they belong. Putting all of the ELL students together and requiring them to "earn their way" into the classes they should be a part of takes away their sense of belonging and damages self-efficacy. The same is true for students who have IEPs. Not only is this not the right solution for students; exclusion also takes away teachers' opportunity to benefit from wider variability in their students. Given the right support to be successful, all teachers can learn to effectively teach all students. But they can't just learn about it and practice on occasion. It has to be part of the classroom routine.

In many schools I visit, I see schools create schedules around the idea of "clustering"—putting students with similar needs into the same homeroom, presumably to be more efficient in delivering intervention. But this clustering practice not only creates equity issues for teachers, it also prevents all teachers from practicing and iterating their inclusive skillset. Coordinated small-group instruction, as shared in Chapter 5, is a logistical solution to ensure classrooms reflect the natural variability in students and yet is responsive to the strengths and needs of each student. This grouping strategy also ensures that all teachers have the chance to stretch their practices and learn from this important experience.

CAN

Playing tennis is something I do in my spare time. I've been playing for more than a decade, but I picked the sport up as an adult. People who have played from the time they were young play differently and with better form. They can execute their skills better. For those who took a long break from playing or those of us who started as adults, there are often skills we *know* but we have trouble carrying out. I know, for example, to follow through on my swing, and yet I regularly forget to do this during a match. I don't need instruction to tell me what to do; I need coaching to help me be able to. This is no different from any skill we learn as adults.

Remember after student teaching how you had just left your teacher preparation program and you were in the know about a lot of practices? You were up to date and ready to begin. You had enthusiasm, but you had not executed many of your skills. This was the time to practice what you knew and become fluent with your new skills. New teachers have often had one or two classes that addressed all of the types of variability you've thought about reading this book. That first year is scary, not from a lack of knowledge, but mostly a lack of being able to apply it in the classroom and honing your craft in the way that you will over the next decades. In this part of Dilt's model, teachers move from knowing the practices that are effective for all students, but they have the ability to apply their knowledge within their own classrooms. At this stage (but not only at this stage), we need a coach to give us feedback and help us apply. The work on instructional coaching is rich—see the work of Jim Knight, Art Costa, and Bob Garmsten for a wealth of information on coaching.

KNOW

Building knowledge of strategies, believe it or not, is one of the easiest components of inclusive change. Schools often ask me to come teach the strategies, and we've certainly explored a lot of strategies in this book. But strategies are relatively easy to learn. Having a required, school-wide professional development session aimed at teaching strategies is not the best way to tackle the need for strategies. We learn best from "just in time" support, not "just in case" support. That is, I learn about strategies to effectively teach students who are lacking a sense of belonging best when I face a student who needs this in my own class. Facilitating professional development that is differentiated and responsive to teachers' own identified strengths and needs is the most efficient and effective approach.

We learn strategies from one another and by engaging in our own self-directed professional learning. Some of the best professional learning comes in the form of visiting one another's classrooms and engaging in dialogue about what's working and what's not working. As an educator, you have areas of expertise—components of your practice that you've developed a great deal of competence and confidence for implementing. Your need is someone else's superpower, and your superpower is someone else's need. Leaders in a school can coordinate the strengths and needs within their faculty body by inviting teachers to self-identify their areas of strength and invite faculty to pair or group with one another for dialogue, intentional classroom visits, and coreflection. For most needs, there is someone in the building who has strengths. And if a pattern of a need arises for which there aren't strengths identified in the building, *then* you've identified a need, perhaps, for additional training or professional development. At this stage, we need a teacher.

REFLECTION

Think about your own strengths and needs within your class this year. What have been your greatest successes? Your greatest challenges? What do you consider to be your superpower—something you have to offer other teachers in your school? What is an area of need you have, and who in the school is really strong in this area?

_____

_____

_____

_____

_____

BELIEVE

A teacher's belief they can be successful in teaching all students is more difficult than learning the strategies. And, yet, a sense of collective self-efficacy is one of the most important elements to a school's success (collective teacher self-efficacy: $d = 1.36$). Collective self-efficacy is a belief of the faculty in the school that they can effectively teach all students at high levels. This goes beyond optimism or the platitude of, "I believe all students can learn." Collective self-efficacy means "I believe we have what it takes to make it happen." Self-efficacy does not mean I believe I have all of the skills or knowledge, but rather I may need some level of support, but I know I can effectively teach all students.

COLLECTIVE TEACHER SELF-EFFICACY

d=1.36

-1.00   0.0   1.50

We all know about the requirement of IDEA of serving students in least restrictive environments. In many ways, though, this is an outdated view of inclusion. This has been a part of the law since the 1970s! I'm not suggesting that we shouldn't serve students in general education classrooms, but rather that including students in the general education classroom isn't enough. And this principle doesn't only apply to students who qualify for an IEP. Remember the "so close and yet so far away" cartoon from Chapter 6 on flexible intervention? Not only does a model of unnecessarily serving students either outside the general education classroom or segregated within a classroom violate the law, but it also harms a classroom teacher's sense of self-efficacy. If, for example, a special education teacher, ELL teacher, or behavior specialist designs and implements all of the intervention, that takes away the classroom teacher's ability to learn new skills and sends the message that the specialist has knowledge and skills that no other teacher can implement.

The way we build self-efficacy in one another as adults is not so different from how we do so with students—we dialogue, reflect together, and mentor one another to success. But to build a real "machine" in our school in which we are engaged in a continuous improvement cycle as a faculty, we have to intentionally build competence and confidence in one another. We need a mentor.

Overlaying this work on coaching, teachers also must consider where and what type of support is needed. Often the default is to think about a student's particular goals and assign that student to an adult who has expertise. But the way we build self-efficacy goes beyond asking what type of support *students* need, and consider what type of support the *adults* need. The frequency and intensity of services a specialist gives to a student is whatever the student needs minus whatever the classroom teacher has. In order to systematically build self-efficacy in one another, before we ever solidify the supports and services a student is to receive, we have to ask the right questions, at the right time (before service decisions are made), about the adults' need for support.

TYPE OF SUPPORT	WHAT THIS MEANS	EXAMPLE
Direct support	I need someone to come into my classroom for now to directly support a group of students. Or the student needs a particular intervention program that I'm not trained to provide.	Ms. Talbert needs a reading specialist to implement Reading Mastery with a group of students. Any student who has a need for this intervention can be a part of the group, not only those who have IEPs.
Coteaching	I need someone to come into my class and teach with me. We can work together to teach all students inclusively.	Ms. Talbert needs a language arts teacher to come into her classroom to teach a writing-heavy unit and teach with her students who need support developing their writing skills.
Modeling	I need someone to come into my classroom to teach me how to provide the support.	Ms. Talbert needs an occupational therapist to come into her class to demonstrate how to help Jayson use a pencil grip with the adapted pencil he has.
Consultation	I need someone to give me advice on a strategy to use.	Ms. Talbert needs a special educator to give her suggestions on how to support Jayson during the stations she has planned for the next unit.
Coaching	I need someone to listen to me and help me find my own solutions to support a student.	Ms. Talbert needs an ELL teacher to talk her through strategies she is using with Maciel. She has worked with a lot of students who are ELL, but she wants to make sure she gets this right.

CASE STORY

While planning the units in her social studies class, Ms. Talbert felt confident in planning for Maciel's support. Ms. Talbert had taught numerous students over the years who spoke Spanish and were new to English. She had learned a wealth of strategies from the ELL teachers she partnered with over the years. Ms. Garcia didn't include as many supports on Maciel's plan because she knew he would be receiving excellent support in Ms. Talbert's class. She planned for mostly coaching and consultation for Maciel in that class. The science teacher, Mr. Barton, though, had less experience with students who were newer to English. Ms. Garcia knew she was going to need to provide more support to Maciel in Mr. Barton's class.

Although Ms. Talbert had high self-efficacy for teaching Maciel, she did not feel the same about designing instruction in a way that supported Jayson. Mx. Brakenstein planned for additional support to Jayson in Ms. Talbert's class but knew this support would fade over time as Ms. Talbert gained new strategies. They knew that Ms. Talbert was enthusiastic about having Jayson in her class and continually worked on making her class more equitable and inclusive. For these reasons, they knew she would be a "quick study."

The IEP team thought through the skills each adult had and asked two question: (1) "What kind of help do we each need to be confident and competent in supporting Jayson?" and (2) "How much do we each need to be confident and competent at supporting Jayson?" These questions lead each teacher to talk about what they would need to feel great about Jayson's learning in their class. Ms. Talbert said she felt great about learning to support Jayson, but she needed help in the beginning. She thought that consultative support where Mx. Brackenstein helped her design units and lessons and find strategies she could use with her whole class was the *type* of support she needed. She thought if they provided that support once or twice a week, that would be enough and she may not need it at all later in the year. Mx. Brackenstein knew they would have to provide some direct instruction with Jayson but also knew that all of Jayson's needs and learning during the day didn't rest solely on their shoulders.

Self-efficacy, like anything else, is not a dichotomy in which you either have it or you don't. It's context dependent. For Ms. Talbert, she had high self-efficacy in teaching students who were newer to the language of instruction than she did teaching students with significant intellectual differences. Ms. Talbert's students, Maciel and Jayson, needed more or less support depending on her own self-efficacy and knowledge in meeting their needs. In other words, the decision about Jayson's support was as much about what Ms. Talbert and the other teachers needed as they are about what Jayson needs. These decisions are transactional, nonlinear, and change over time.

IDENTIFY

Not all teachers identify as teachers of all students. I still hear teachers say "my students" and "your students." The implication is that students who need specialized support by a counselor, special educator, ELL teacher, reading specialist, etc. *belong* to those. This is the opposite of an inclusive approach, and this fractured approach to instruction and support undermines any approach to inclusion. It is absolutely necessary that teachers identify as inclusive teachers. Before those of you who are specialists get excited about this—this pertains to you as well. Calling students on your caseload "my students," or worse, "my babies," does not make this better! First, it perpetuates the idea that some students do not belong to their classroom teachers. Second, calling students "babies" infantilizes a group of students who are likely already at risk for marginalization. Specialists are teachers of all students, too. And you accomplish this by providing support to other adults, thus impacting all students. Teachers who don't identify as teachers of all students need a sponsor who says "I see you this way; let me show you." Leaders have a responsibility in this identity as well. In your hiring practices, understanding where candidates are in their identity as teachers of all students is critical to your mission of inclusion.

Some years ago in my role as a professor in a college of education, our dean asked us to self-identify our areas of expertise. This way when the media or a school called, he could connect them to a professor who had expertise to answer their questions or provide support. School leaders can do the same: ask teachers to identify their areas of expertise. Publish this grid so when a teacher has a need, they can get the "just in time" professional learning by visiting another teacher's class with intention. Teachers, don't be shy to own an area of expertise. Even the newest teacher has important contributions to offer.

LEAD

The foundational and most important component of this nested model is for a school to lead a mission of inclusion. Mission is far more than a mission statement on a website or in a document—it requires leadership. Many of us don't even know the mission and vision statements after they are developed. When a school really has a mission of inclusion, it is the ethos of the school—it's who they *are*. We can get a sense of the ethos of a school by taking a look at what they celebrate. Is there a lot of emphasis on class rank, who is the valedictorian based on a GPA, or an honor roll that is based on academic achievement? When you walk in the front of the building, what is the evidence of what is celebrated? Many times the front of the building has trophy cases for athletic talent and achievement. I've even seen halls with banners that named the students who scored "proficient" or "distinguished" on state exams. There is nothing wrong with celebrating academic achievement, but when it is the main or only significant celebration, schools are not showing that they have inclusive values. Inclusive schools celebrate the whole child.

A student new to the language of instruction may not excel on academic standards right away but is both incredibly engaged in school and persistent learning a new language. A student with a learning disability may need support with reading but has sophisticated thinking skills. A student who is not confident in math and requires intervention may be an amazing communicator with the ability to lead a group to resolve conflict. The student who has experienced significant trauma may find many classes to take too much of a cognitive load but finds art to be a release and shows outstanding creativity. Some students may feel as if they don't belong or "fit in" except in a sport with a community of athletes and shines as a leader in that environment.

This ethos can be the most difficult change for a school to make. For this stage we need a leader. Although realizing this mission is the responsibility of everyone in the building, and really everyone in the community, it's the school leaders and school boards who set this tone.

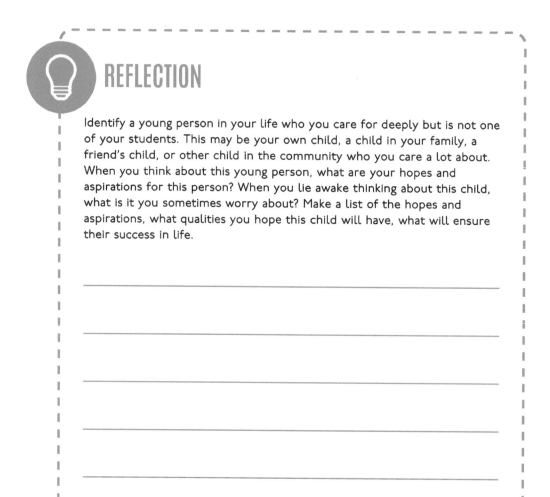

REFLECTION

Identify a young person in your life who you care for deeply but is not one of your students. This may be your own child, a child in your family, a friend's child, or other child in the community who you care a lot about. When you think about this young person, what are your hopes and aspirations for this person? When you lie awake thinking about this child, what is it you sometimes worry about? Make a list of the hopes and aspirations, what qualities you hope this child will have, what will ensure their success in life.

I remember when my older child was in first grade. He was the lowest reader in the class. And in most grades, students who had the highest academic achievements were given awards. You remember this from your time in school: the highest grades in academic and performance-based subjects. The awards are less often about skills that honor the broad variability in our students and the strengths that each one brings. My child's first grade teacher knew her students well. She recognized the strengths that each student had and celebrated these. In the awards ceremony at the end of the year, my child got the award for "the best questions asked." And, you know what? That's still true today! This wasn't a token award, but rather one that recognized and valued a quality in him that was beyond the academic standards. Going beyond academic standards to value the excellence each student offers is equitable and inclusive. That's what it's all about. The extent to which we define achievement in a standard way that excludes the recognition of the variety of incredible strengths in each student is the extent to which we don't care about equity and inclusion. If we truly care about and value having an ethos of equity and inclusiveness, we have an urgent call to disrupt the ways of the past.

SUMMARY

When we think about what we want the children in our lives to become—we see a vision for their life, if you will. The young person's GPA is rarely at the heart of what we envision. It probably didn't even make your list. We usually care most about what schools celebrate the least. We all, of course, value reading, communication, problem-solving, and other transfer skills explicitly taught and assessed in school. But in your reflections, you probably had more thoughts around empathy, interaction, questioning, creativity, persistence, critical thinking, conflict resolution, self-regulation, confidence, and you get the idea. But life for our young people, both inside and outside the walls of the school, is often emotionally unsafe. There is all too often inequity in opportunities for students to develop and shine in each of these ways we all value. The world around us categorizes humans and "plays favorites." We have to work diligently to ever improve in our efforts to ensure that these inequities in the world are not reflected in our schools—a task that is complex, ever evolving, and never finished.

But thoughtful and intentional design of our classrooms, curriculum, instruction, and assessment with intention to bring equity and inclusion changes lives. We can open doors for students to know they are seen, valued, heard, and ultimately not only perform well in academic pursuits, but in *life* pursuits. We can equip every student to engage with confidence, have an intense desire to learn, plan for their own learning, and know what strategies work for them. Each adult within a school has a moral responsibility to see the complete picture of who their students are, what they will become, and our role in making their world as big as it possibly can be. The part teachers play in this work is first to value, empower, and support students, with equity and inclusion at the forefront of every single decision we make. We have to make intentional choices about how we represent the broad range of human characteristics in our classrooms, the warm and kind interactions we offer, the ways we support all students to understand what they are learning, and invite students to express their learning in the ways that give power to their strengths. These decisions are at the heart of realizing the visions we hold, not for most students, but for *each* student. Focusing squarely and exclusively on a single view of teaching academic standards and only to a mythical average is like looking at an old newspaper comic strip from three inches away. When your eyes are that close, all you see are dots. It could do us all well to "zoom" out farther and farther from this close-up view to see the whole picture of each student. And what a spectacularly beautiful picture it is!

 ## SELF-ASSESSMENT

I can reflect on the initiatives my school has taken on in recent years and identify patterns of these initiatives that "stuck."	
I can use Dilt's nested levels of logic to reflect on where my school is to determine my needs and the needs of my school.	
I can facilitate discussion and decision-making around the type of support that adults need, including my own, to carry out UDL and intervention.	

References

Amerikaner, A. S. (2012). *Unequal education federal loophole enables lower spending on students of color*. Center for American Progress. https://cdn.uncf.org/wp-content/uploads/PDFs/UnequalEduation.pdf

Arias, B. (2007). School desegregation, linguistic segregation and access to English for Latino students. *Journal of Educational Controversy, 2*(1), Article 7. https://cedar.wwu.edu/jec/vol2/iss1/7

Bandura, A. (1994). Self-efficacy. In V. S. Ramachaudran (Ed.), *Encyclopedia of human behavior* (Vol. 4, pp. 71–81). Academic Press.

Berk, L. E. (2003). *Child development*. Allyn and Bacon.

Black, P. (2013). Formative and summative aspects of assessment: Theoretical and research foundations in the context of pedagogy. In J. H. McMillan (Ed.), *SAGE handbook of research on classroom assessment* (pp. 167–178). SAGE Publications, Inc. https://doi.org/10.4135/9781452218649.n10

Black, P., & Wiliam, D. (1998). Assessment and classroom learning. *Assessment in Education: Principles, Policy & Practice, 5*(1), 7–68.

Burgess, A. W., Garbarino, C., & Carlson, M. I. (2006). Pathological teasing and bullying turned deadly: Shooters and suicide. *Victims & Offenders, 1*(1), 1–14.

Burns, M. K., Barrett, C. A., Maki, K. E., Hajovsky, D. B., Duesenberg, M. D., & Romero, M. E. (2020). Recommendations in school psychological evaluation reports for academic deficits: Frequency, types, and consistency with student data. *Contemporary School Psychology, 24*(4), 478–487.

Butler, R. (1988). Enhancing and undermining intrinsic motivation; the effects of task-involving and ego-involving evaluation on interest and performance. *British Journal of Educational Psychology, 58*(1), 1–14.

Butler, R., & Nisan, M. (1986). Effects of no feedback, task-related comments, and grades on intrinsic motivation and performance. *Journal of Educational Psychology, 78*, 210–216.

Deci, & Ryan, R. M. (Eds.). (2002). *Handbook of self-determination research* (pp. 3–33). University of Rochester Press.

Deci, E. L., Ryan, R. M., & Williams, G. C. (1996). Need satisfaction and the self-regulation of learning. *Learning and Individual Differences, 8*, 165–183.

Dweck, C. S. (2000). *Self-theories: Their role in motivation, personality and development*. Psychology Press.

Ehmer, M. R. (2018). Teacher identity and the role of relational coaching. *Open Access Dissertations*, 1718.

Elawar, M. C., & Corno, L. (1985). A factorial experiment in teachers' written feedback on student homework: Changing teacher behavior a little rather than a lot. *Journal of Educational Psychology, 77*, 162–173.

Evans, M., & Boucher, A. (2015). Optimizing the power of choice: Supporting student autonomy to foster motivation and engagement in learning. *Mind, Brain, and Education, 9*. https://doi.org/10.1111/mbe.12073

Flowerday, T., & Schraw, G. (2000). Teacher beliefs about instructional choice: A phenomenological study. *Journal of Educational Psychology, 92*(4), 634–645.

FPG Child Development Institute, University of North Carolina at Chapel Hill. (2007, Spring). RTI goes to Pre-K: An early intervening system called recognition & response. *Early Developments, 11*(1), 6–10.

Garmston, R. J., & Wellman, B. M. (2016). In *The adaptive school: A sourcebook for* developing collaborative groups (3rd ed.). Rowman and Littlefield Publishers.

Gershenson, S., Holt, S. B., & Papageorge, N. W. (2015). *Who believes in me? The effect of student-teacher demographic match on teacher expectations.* Upjohn Institute Working Paper 15-231. W.E. Upjohn Institute for Employment Research. http://dx.doi.org/10.17848/wp15-231

Giangreco, M. F. (2004). "The stairs didn't go anywhere!": A self-advocate's reflections on specialized services and their impact on people with disabilities. In M. Nind, J. Rix, K. Sheehy, & K. Simmons (Eds.), *Inclusive education: Diverse perspectives* (pp. 32–42). David Fulton Publishers in association with The Open University.

Giangreco, M. F., Shogren, K. A., & Dymond, S. K. (2020). Educating students with severe disabilities: Foundational concepts and practices. In F. Brown, J. McDonnell, & M. E. Snell (Eds.), *Instruction of students with severe disabilities: Meeting the needs of children and youth with intellectual disabilities, multiple disabilities, and autism spectrum disorders* (9th ed., pp. 1–27). Pearson.

Giangreco, M. F., Yuan, S., McKenzie, B., Cameron, P., & Fialka, J. (2005). "Be careful what you wish for...": Five reasons to be concerned about the assignment of individual paraprofessionals. *Teaching Exceptional Children, 37*(5), 28–34.

Haring, N., Liberty, K., & White, O. (1976). *First annual report: Field initiated research studies of phases of learning and facilitating instructional events for the severely/ profoundly handicapped.* (U.S. Department of Education, Contract No. G0075 00593). University of Washington, College of Education.

Hattie, J. (2016). https://www.visible learningmetax.com/Influences

Hidi, S., & Renninger, K. A. (2006). The four-phase model of interest development. *Educational Psychologist, 41*, 111–127.

Individuals with disabilities education act, 20 U.S.C. § 1400. (2004).

Joshi, G. S., & Bouck, E. C. (2017). Examining postsecondary education predictors and participation for students with learning disabilities. *Journal of Learning Disabilities, 50*(1), 3–13. https://doi.org/10.1177/0022219415572894

Lewis, L. K. (1998). The influence of external factors in the overrepresentation of African American males in Minnesota special education programs. *Theses and Graduate Projects, 731.*

Lipnevich, A., & Smith, J. (2009). Effects of differential feedback on students' examination performance. *Journal of Experimental Psychology: Applied, 15*(4), 319–333.

McDonald, J. H. (2014). In *Handbook of biological statistics* (3rd ed.). Sparky House Publishing.

McMaster, K. L., Fuchs, D., & Fuchs, L. S. (2006). Research on peer-assisted learning strategies: The promise and limitations of peer-mediated instruction. *Reading & Writing Quarterly, 22*(1), 5–25.

National Center for Learning Disabilities. (2020). *Significant disproportionality in special education: Current trends and actions for impact.* https://www.ncld.org/wp-content/uploads/2020/10/2020-NCLD-Disproportionality_Trends-and-Actions-for-Impact_FINAL-1.pdf

National Center on Response to Intervention. (March 2010). *Essential components of RTI—a closer look at response to intervention.* U.S. Department of Education, Office of Special Education Programs, National Center on Response to Intervention.

National Council on Disability. (2018). *(IDEA series) the segregation of students with disabilities.* https://ncd.gov/sites/default/files/NCD_Segregation-SWD_508.pdf

O'Connor, R. E., Bocian, K., Beach, K., & Sanchez, T. (2014). Access to a responsiveness to intervention model: Does beginning intervention in kindergarten matter? *Journal of Learning Disabilities, 47*, 307–328.

Otis, N., Grouzet, F. M. E., & Pelletier, L. G. (2005). Latent motivational change in an academic setting: A 3-year longitudinal study. *Journal of Educational Psychology, 97*, 170–183. https://doi.org/10.1037/0022-0663.97.2.170

Palmer, D., & Archer. (2016). Using situational interest to enhance individual interest and science-related behaviours, *Research in Science Education, 47*, 731–753.

Patall, E., Cooper, H., & Wynn, S. R. (2010). The effectiveness and relative importance of choice in the classroom. *Journal of Educational Psychology, 102*, 896–915. https://doi.org/10.1037/a0019545

Perkins, D. N., & Salomon, G. (1989). Are cognitive skills context-bound? *Educational Research, 18*, 16–25.

Pierson, R. F. (2013). *Every kid needs a champion* [Video]. TED.

Posey, A. (2019). *Engage the brain*. ASCD.

Purkey, W. W., & Novak, J. M. (1996). *Inviting school success: A self-concept approach to teaching, learning, and democratic practice* (3rd ed.). Wadsworth Publishing.

Ralabate, P. (2016). *Your UDL lesson planner: The step-by-step guide for teaching all learners*. Brookes Publishing.

Roediger, H. L. (1980). Memory metaphors in cognitive psychology. *Memory & Cognition, 8*(3), 231–246.

Rose, T. (2016). *The end of average*. Harper Collins.

Rotter, J. B. (1954). *Social learning and clinical psychology*. Prentice-Hall.

Rotter, J. B. (1966). Generalized expectancies for internal versus external control of reinforcement. *Psychological Monographs: General and Applied, 80*(1), 1.

Shogren, K. A., Faggella-Luby, M. N., Jik, S., & Wehmeyer, M. L. (2004). The effect of choice-making as an intervention for problem behavior: A meta-analysis. *Journal of Positive Behavior Interventions, 6*(4), 228–237. https://doi.org/10.1177/10983007040060040401

Suliman, S., Mkabile, S. G., Fincham, D. S., Ahmed, R., Stein, D. J., & Seedat, S. (2009). Cumulative effect of multiple trauma on symptoms of posttraumatic stress disorder, anxiety, and depression in adolescents. *Comprehensive Psychiatry, 50*(2), 121–127. https://doi.org/10.1016/j.comppsych.2008.06.006

Tanner, K. D. (2012). Approaches to biology teaching and learning: Promoting student metacognition, *Life Sciences Education, 11*, 113–120.

The Trevor Project. (2021). *2021 National survey on LGBTQ youth mental health*. The Trevor Project.

Tomlinson, C. A. (2014). *The differentiated classroom: Responding to the needs of all learners* (2nd ed.). ASCD.

Torgesen, J. K. (2004). Lessons learned from research on interventions for students who have difficulty learning to read. In P. McCardle & V. Chhabra (Eds.), *The voice of evidence in reading research* (pp. 355–382). Paul H. Brookes Publishing Co, Inc.

UNCF. (2022). K-12 *Disparity Facts and Statistics*. UNCF. https://uncf.org/pages/k-12-disparity-facts-and-stats

US Department of Education, Office of Civil Rights. (2014). *Civil rights data snapshot: College and career readiness*. https://cdn.uncf.org/wp-content/uploads/PDFs/CRDC-College-and-Career-Readiness-Snapshot-2.pdf

Wanzek, J., & Vaughn, S. (2007). Research-based implications from extensive early reading interventions. *School Psychology Review, 36*(4), 541–561.

Wiliam, D. (2016). The secret of effective feedback. *Educational Leadership, 73*(7).

https://www.ascd.org/el/articles/the-secret-of-effective-feedback

Zimmerman, B. J. (2001). Theories of self-regulated learning and academic achievement: An overview and analysis. In B. J. Zimmerman & D. H. Schunk (Eds.), *Self-regulated learning and academic achievement: Theoretical perspectives* (pp. 1–65). Lawrence Erlbaum Associates Publishers.

Index

A SAGE Publishing Company

CORWIN HAS ONE MISSION: to enhance education through intentional professional learning. We build long-term relationships with our authors, educators, clients, and associations who partner with us to develop and continuously improve the best evidence-based practices that establish and support lifelong learning.

lead inclusion.
all students are OUR students.

all students are OUR students.

The Lead Inclusion team provides educators with support and practical, research-based strategies in the areas of universal design, inclusive education, and mastery assessment.

DR. LEE ANN JUNG
Educator, Author, Consultant

Dr. Lee Ann Jung is the founder of Lead Inclusion and a consultant, author, and speaker for schools worldwide. Lee Ann supports schools in the areas of universal design for learning, inclusion, intervention, and mastery assessment and grading. In her nearly 30 years in the field of education, she has served in the roles of teacher, administrator, researcher, consultant, and professor. She is a clinical professor at San Diego State University and a former professor and director of international partnerships at University of Kentucky. Follow her on Twitter at @leeannjung.

COURSES

Choose between a variety of courses either facilitated by an instructor on-site or online, or self-paced online. Courses include online modules with slides, videos, readings, and supplemental content.

INCLUSION REVIEW

Looking through the lenses of UDL and inclusion, we lead in-depth reviews of teaching environments, policies, and instruction to identify strengths and areas to target.

CONSULTING & PROFESSIONAL DEVELOPMENT

Contact us to learn how our team can work shoulder-to-shoulder with you in furthering efforts in UDL, inclusion, assessment, or grading.

Visit leadinclusion.org to learn more.

CORWIN

EQ2264250